THE ART OF MOTORCYCLE HAIKU

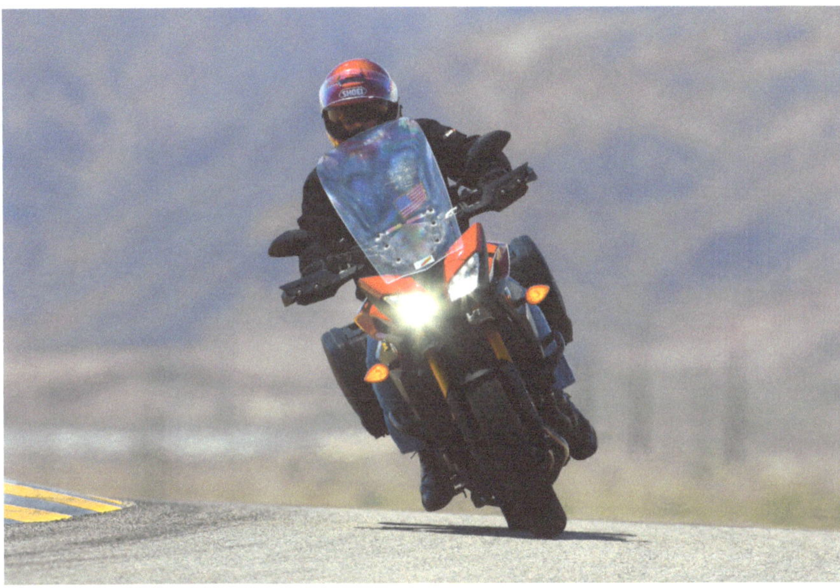

MARK FARGO

Other books by Mark Fargo

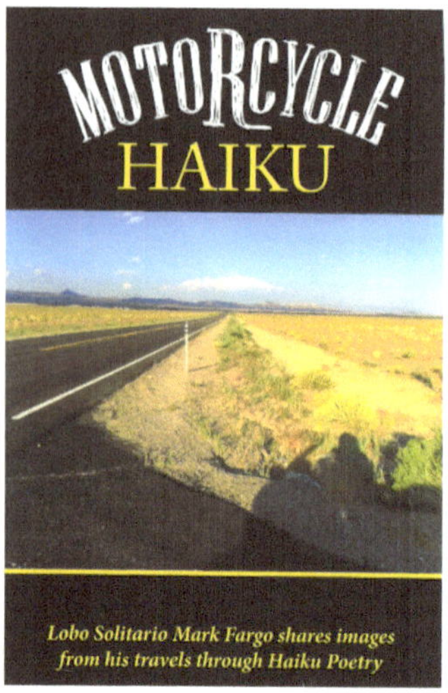

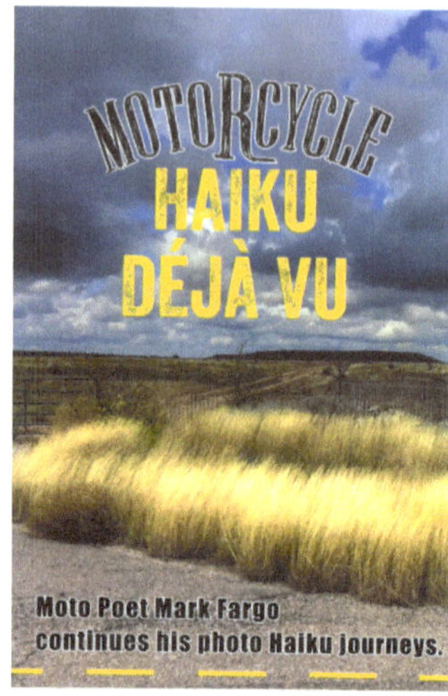

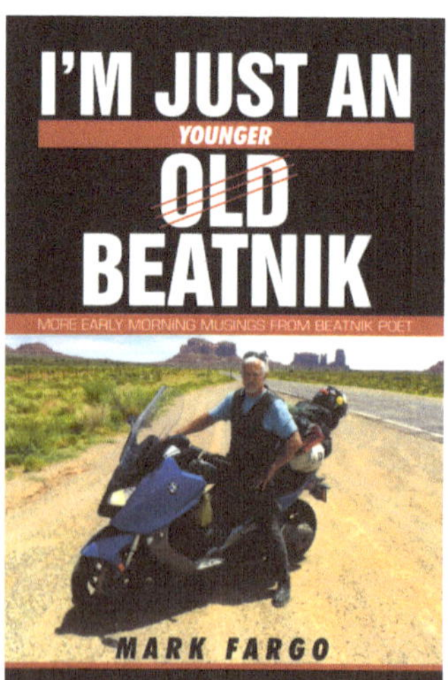

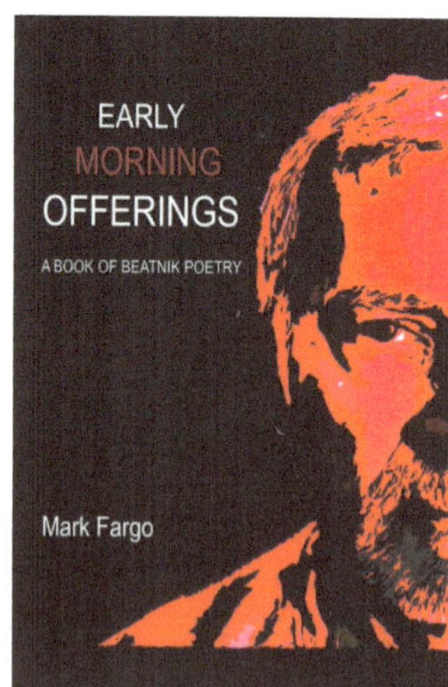

THE ART OF MOTORCYCLE HAIKU

MARK FARGO

LONE WOLF PRINTS

ISBN 978-0-578-44704-9

Book Design by Blue Jay Ink
Ojai, California
bluejayink.com

Published in the United States by
Lone Wolf Prints

LONE WOLF PRINTS

markfargo.com

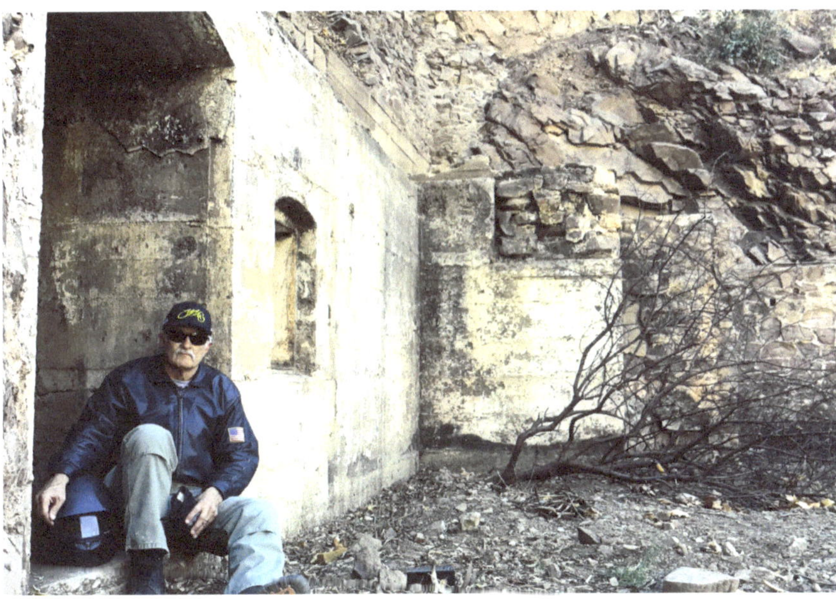

Moto Poet: A lone traveler who combines photography and poetry to record his journeys.

Dedication

To my neighbor, friend and Motorcycle Haiku series book guru, Frank Boross, (aka toxic coyote) who became ill over the holidays in 2017 and passed shortly after of liver cancer. Our political discussions, organizational skills and suggestive creative inputs will be missed by many, especially me. Lobo Solitario will think of you often, while I am on the road and when I see that lone coyote in those hills, or streams or byways scavenging to get by. Rest peacefully in your new den.

Tanka for Frank

Toxic coyote
Loved his sauerkraut dogs
Hated Tic Tac Trump
Mars Attack all time movie
Hawaiian shirt/shorts his suits

And to Sergio Rodriguez, who served in the Marine Corps, loved motorcycles and helping others . He was the manager of Cycle Gear in Oxnard where he passed away suddenly at work at age 39. He is survived by his three children who he adored and his loving wife Kristi. RIP

#841

Mechanic mindset
Wife Kristi three kids he loved
Canyon rides for fun
Racing oval kiss the curves
Generous heart missed by all

Prologue

My philosophy regarding motorcycle travel, photography, and the simplicity of my daily adventures is the motivating factor for my Lobo Solitario approach to being on the road. I travel alone by choice and not having an agenda allows me to move in any direction at any time. I try not to back track and believe if I missed something, I'll catch it next time.

I don't consider myself a photographer, but rather a recorder of daily life from my motorcycle. I use an iPad 6 to record my images. Its advanced lens and various settings make my transition from bike to the location of the shot effortlessly. It also has a typing pad with a military hard case for the occasional ground-pounding landing, so I can make notes and record locations later on. I see the world on my rides and want you to ride along with me. Some question the use of this technology instead of the usual digital or more expensive camera, but I don't photoshop or manipulate my images, because I think it's important that you see just what I see.

For those familiar with my previous work, *Motorcycle Haiku* and *Motorcycle Haiku Déjà Vu*, this will be a familiar format for you. If you're experiencing my travels for the first time, please enjoy the ride. I hope you become a loyal follower of my road trips.

Photography with technology is photo art, not pure photography. No judgment here, but for what I do, sometimes traveling hundreds of miles at a time and getting off my ride several times a day, I want to keep the situation simple and not spend hours trying to enhance my images. What you see is what I saw. In addition to the hard copy book, I do recommend that you purchase the electronic version for a minimal fee, as the electronic version offers better photo images - perfect print reproduction of the photos is almost impossible. Some have told me that they buy both the paperback because it's affordable and hey, they still like holding a book in their hands.

I don't own a car so I get the opportunity to enjoy all the elements of travel, including rain, severe winds and chaotic traffic conditions, and put them into play every day. I am gifted with good health and when required, the wisdom of driving defensively, keeping myself safe from those using technology while they drive. It's more the norm now than eating, putting on makeup, speeding, drinking or God forbid, combinations of any of the above.

I grew up in the Stand by Me small town of Oak View, California, halfway between Ventura and Ojai. Coming from Los Angeles, my childhood years were spent flying kites, digging fox holes with my brother Cary, and putting coins or rocks on the train track, which was one hundred feet from our backyard fence. I also spent hours riding my lime green butterfly handlebars, white tuck and roll seat Schwinn Stingray, which I earned and bought myself as a ten-year-old delivering the LA Times from the back of my dad's open rear door (not legal now) Mercury station wagon.

The Thomas Fire of 2017, here in Ventura County, California, had a permanent effect on me concerning the fragility of life. I knew people who lost their homes but luckily none who lost their lives. The floods in Santa Barbara and off Highway 33 outside of Ojai were shocking and disheartening. I was a quarter mile away from evacuating. As a resident of Ventura for most of my life, I have been through a lot of natural disasters. Earthquakes, fires, droughts and floods, not to mention how the booming population of this state and its human impact have changed my daily behavior forever. The Thomas Fire was just the start of the massive and destructive fire season that spread all the way up to Vancouver, Canada. The jet stream helped contribute to some very poor visibility days on this trip. The smoke basically just went east from the west coast, sometimes being sighted in the Midwest and beyond.

The first five days from my Portland departure on August 21, 2018, was spent in poor visibility smoke-filled skies, which led to a disappointing start with limited photo opportunities. I never clearly saw the Canadian Rockies and missed riding the famed Going-to-the-Sun Road out of the west entrance of Glacier National Park. It rained when I was camping near Lake Louise, and the air never really cleared enough to fully appreciate my surroundings. One of the few clear shots I got was when I was leaving Banff along a glacier stream and railroad tracks. It will be obvious when you see it in the book. It is a stunning view and demonstrates the relationship between rivers and railroad tracks.

Without recording anybody's personal loss from the foothills of Ventura, I have decided to include a brief reminder of that tragic period and the effects of our state's second largest wildfire. This includes a few photographs with one Tanka poem, (5-7-5-7-7 syllables), which in traditional Japanese Haiku format, addresses sorrow or loss. Some of you may have seen some of these posted over the past two years -- one reason why I still travel three to four months a year is to record life and the environment we live in.

The Thomas Fire, in a way, made me realize that at any time our lives can change quickly and dramatically. Now sixty-five years old, I realize how living for the day is a smart and best practice. As an advocate for preserving the environment, many times I have seen people who are left hopeless from a natural event that has occurred. I understand that fires are part of the earth's recycling program, just like hurricanes, floods and tornadoes. Humankind should not participate in that process.

P.S. I would also like to thank all of you for participation in deciding what the cover of my third Haiku book would be. I gave you many choices from many different locations from many different states and all of those choices will be in the book itself with their Haiku, so anyone who didn't have their favorite landscape picked for the cover will still see it in the book.

Please enjoy my third installment of the Motorcycle Haiku series with all its images, poetry, and comments that have affected me on every trip I've taken. I am blessed.

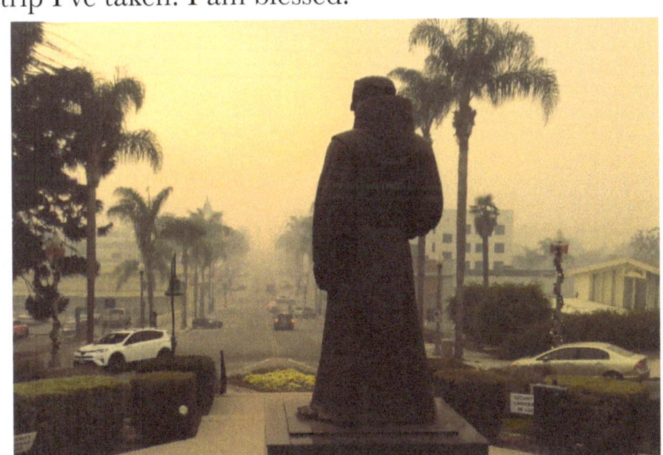

Father Serra looking over smoke-filled downtown Ventura post Thomas Fire.

Scorched

Bark-less tree naked
Nest-less bird all charred branches
Crispy rolling hills
Incinerated species
Cycle of life recycling

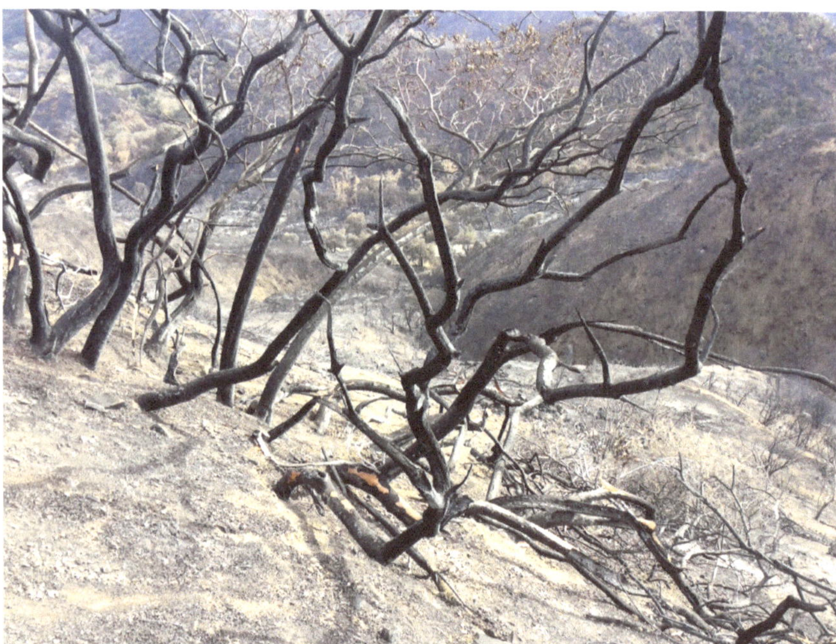

California has turned into a tinder box. Highway 33, one of my favorite local rides, was not spared. Almost 1.7 million acres have been burned this fire season, in 2018, including the most human loss of life, The Paradise Fire.

What is Motorcycle Haiku?

I am often asked what Motorcycle Haiku is because there is not much information regarding the subject matter. To my knowledge, I believe that I was the pioneer back in 2016, combining Haiku poetry with the sheer joy of cross country motorcycling and photographs from my daily travels.

What makes this a unique genre is the combination of traditional Haiku poetry, photography and motorcycling. Traditional Haiku poetry, originating in Japan, addresses the four seasons of change using seventeen syllables, usually three phrases of five, seven and five syllables, in non-rhyming verse. There have been several well-known traditional Haiku poets, and this form of poetry often includes two pictures.

Almost every Haiku uses a key word that refers to the specific season, making it easy for the reader to discern the season presented. The key word is more of a cue so that the reader can recall his/her own memories and references, sometimes nostalgic, of the season. Can one not feel the early colder mornings and evenings that are signaling the coming of the fall season? Or how after months of rain during the winter, blooming flowers announce that the spring season has arrived?

This mystical awareness from Zen Buddhism masters was first introduced to Haiku by Basho in the mid 1600's, followed by Buson in the early 1700's, who was less interested in the mystical relationship and more in vignettes and third, Issa, in the mid 1700's, who was more humorous and individualistic. A fourth, Shiki, from the mid 1800's, gave the world a more modern Buson, and viewed the art form as one to give more perfectly accountable glimpses to everyday circumstances, regardless of the season.

After looking at all their work, and without prior knowledge of it, I see myself more like Shiki, as I travel with no set schedule, regardless of the time of year. Being a Californian and with the seemingly changing climate that we are all experiencing, I am fortunate to be able to travel year-round, as I can always head east to Arizona or New Mexico in the late fall and catch very ridable weather without all the recreational vehicles and occasionally obnoxious tourists from other countries. I especially enjoy the fall season on the west coast as we rarely experience much rain before the holidays -- Highway 1, the national parks and the deserts are all accessible and produce more enjoyable rides with less traffic.

The major factor that makes my Haiku unique is that I simply look at each day as a new adventure and without pressuring myself to get some great shots. I just go about my business of enjoying the hypnotic guttural symphony emanating from my Yamaha Super Tenere hitting the road. I am not looking for any shot in particular and many times it is something that catches my eye peripherally or just due to a chance glance. The cover of my second book, "Motorcycle Haiku Déjà Vu," was from just a glimpse of a golden ring standing out against the darkening and cloudy skies to my right. I had to travel a bit so that I could legally swing back to get the shot.

Some people ask me why I don't photograph more iconic shots that many people already know. My response is simply that with hundreds of thousands of famous shots of famous places, another one from me would just add to the deluge and in the end, just be another shot. I am not saying that I go out of my way to avoid opportunities for famous shots, rather I feel that they have already been done and I like to think that my photography piques people's curiosity. "Where did you take that Mark?" A lot of times it is within miles of their own destination.

I find myself looking for unique shots, sometimes just outside a national park like one I took of the Merced River outside of Yosemite. I heard the river roaring from the twenty-car line I was behind and just pulled over. I spent a good half hour getting a little wet to get the shot I chose. I'm in the dirt, hiking, and sometimes waiting for longs periods of time for my shots. It's always worth it.

Motorcycle Haiku is the daily journey, the distractions, the challenges I face every day. It may not meet traditional standards nor expectations; one Haiku journal reviewer said my Haiku was too choppy to meet his standards, but Motorcycle Haiku is not to be compared to traditional Haiku. Motorcycle Haiku simply uses its format to address the journey and photographs that happen along the way. Sometimes I use the thirty-one syllable Tanka format if it is applicable to the shot taken. Bottom line: I love to ride this country with its two-lane highways, rural country folk and blue-plate specials and to get lost discovering all of them. I'll keep riding until I no longer feel safe out there. Presently, I am not interested in the two back tires, one front tire motorcycle-size transportation. I like just two wheels. I also like to wear long pants, motorcycle hard toe boots and padded jackets and a full helmet, which I will address next.

To Helmet or Not to Helmet?

Over the years and many adventures across America, in diners, gas stations, bars (with beers), BBQs and living rooms, this topic of discussion has, sometimes heated with expletives and hurt feelings, divided friends and acquaintances, similar to our country's current political tribal culture.

Shall we blame the furor on technology or the money that controls our political systems? Certainly not hospitals, missing their free donors, or advanced safety practices. As a retired high school social science teacher and DMV handbook-only driver's education instructor, whose sole purpose is to get the kids prepared to take the test, I can honestly say that technology is one of the main culprits behind motorcycle fatalities, the other being speed and bad choices from the under-thirty crowd. Coming from California, a state that offers some of the most scenic rides in America, a state that has over 800,000 registered two-wheel fun-loving enthusiasts and the only state that allows lane-splitting (much to the dismay of many four wheeled owners), I can live with wearing a helmet.

In California, you have lots of different helmet choices. For example, there is the "open face brain bucket," which I assume earned its name because it is easier to scoop up your brains after a high-speed crash or even just a bad skid. There is also the "full face with shield," which I prefer over any other type if it is DOT (Department of Transportation) approved. I usually ride with a helmet that has a Snell certification as well because it is tested at a higher-level crash test procedure. You've only got one mug, so why have a rock, bird or any other flying object rearrange it? One EMT in New Mexico told me the story of a no-helmet rider, who for some unknown reason flew off the back of his bike and hit the pavement hard. When they turned him over there was a quarter size rock implanted between his eyes. End of story. Depending on the speed of impact, that incident would just ding or crack my Snell-certified helmet, not shatter it or knock me off my ride.

In 1992, with its ever-increasing number of new riders, more accidents and concerns generated from scraping brains off the pavement, California enacted a helmet law. Before 1992, regardless of the state in which they rode, motorcyclists were often referred to simply as organ donors, due to their frequent fatal accidents that resulted in their organs becoming available to others. The outrage emanating from the law was predictable, of course, from the Easy Rider generation, from misplaced 1st Amendments rights advocates and perhaps from the hospitals, who were about to lose a fair amount of freebies to their donor base, despite the horror stories from the ER crews. Outside of the gunshot wounds and car accidents that are often inflicted on motorcyclists, riders now had to conform to a new law which impeded the wind flowing through their hair and their cool good looks, not to mention affecting the outlaw clubs of high school dropouts, which upset many. Think about it --- who rode motorcycles and why back then is open to debate, but many people assumed the riders were misfits, rebels, anti-establishment types and non-college graduates who carried illegal switch blades and didn't bathe regularly. I'm guilty of the latter two occasionally, but the message is to pay attention to where you are as the laws vary from state to state.

Personally, I am at the point where after all the whining from non-helmet state riders I have met over my adventures, I believe that there should not be a helmet law. What you saying, Lobo? You're from the nanny state of California, which caresses and coddles every one of the thirty-nine million people who live there and the thousands who visit here every day. The state is so politically correct that it makes people from elsewhere either envious of us or just plain hate us because of our great topography, Hollywood, wine tasting, innovation and of course, great weather.

In my anti-helmet position, I am not against 1st Amendment rights or free speech, but offering a simple solution that I think would nevertheless still cause distress and rising temperatures. I say give riders the choice but meet the following conditions:

1. If you choose not to wear a helmet, you must carry full insurance.

2. Your license has an automatic donor notification label, (making hospitals very happy again).

3. No one in your family can sue for malpractice in your ER visit if you end up drooling in a wheelchair the rest of your life. ER doctors say there is only so much you can do when you show up with half a brain. These conditions satisfy all 1st Amendment advocates and most importantly supports personal responsibility for your actions.

Why I Travel Alone (Lobo Solitario)

Inevitably, with almost a hundred percent surety, when I mention that I ride a motorcycle, people will say, "Oh, you're a biker." In response to that image of a person riding without a helmet, his or her hair flowing like a convoluted fan screaming off their unprotected head, possibly or most likely an unshaven face, on a two-lane highway in the desert with a sullen disposition, my automatic response is, "No, I'm a motorcyclist." Responses vary of course, some just "oohing" in their teasing manner and others flatly saying, "What's the difference?" To me there is a really big difference. Before I address this two-classification genre I would like to explain how I got to this conclusion. A brief family history here is warranted.

My ideology, or in everyday terms, my mindset, peers back to that era of independence and adventure when people first thought people like me had an exciting and without question, dangerous choice of transportation. There was that free spirit that people envied and admired along with their inner thoughts of horrid wrecks and stories ending with organ donors.

Gone are the days of kick-starting your ride, simple motors you could work on with a few Craftsman tools, small size motors (a 650 cc was a monster bike sixty years ago) no electronics whatsoever and certainly no safety features. I've only been on the open road for five years. I am glad I am a late bloomer. I had no impulse control as a teenager, with no regard for speed or concern for others if they rode in my car. My first car, a forest green 56 Chevy with a 283 Vet engine, reverse linkage (short life expectancy as it was my first on the floor shifter), was one I purchased myself in high school and quickly blew up, seeing how fast I could go on the back-frontage roads of Ventura, CA. I got my five hundred dollars' worth.

My parents had the insight to advise me from a very early age that if I wanted anything that was that important to me, I should be the one buying it. I always had a job to pay for the gas and insurance and could make my own decisions. This parenting education, i.e., if you want it that badly you need to work for it, started in the sixties, when I was ten and living in that Stand by Me town of Oak View California, just north of Ventura. I wanted a new style bicycle, a Schwinn, called the Sting Ray. It was the newest, ultimate bike, with its knobby tires, butterfly handlebars, white tuck-and-roll seat and for me, needed to be in the cool lime green color. At Christmas I mentioned to my dad that he could forget about wasting his money on me for a Pendleton shirt, Levi's or the latest game and get me this bike. My dad, who came from nothing himself as a kid and had a cantankerous father, did not hesitate and responded, "I suggest you get a job." After I picked up my jaw and heart, I got the stare and then got the best thing my dad did for me in the lessons-for-life moments of my young life. "If anything you want is that important to you, then you should buy it yourself, so it has value and you will take care of it." I was just ten innocent years old and he wants me to get a job? Really? He mentioned that I could mow lawns, paint address numbers on curbs or deliver papers. I chose the latter and to my dad's credit, he helped me. After watching me fold all the papers at four am, he would drive me in his Mercury station wagon as I threw the Sunday LA Times from the open fold, down gates and driveways for six months until I got the sixty-five bucks to buy the bike. I then was treated to a Cuddles Donut, usually a sprinkled cake, one of my favorites, as he flirted with its owner, Hazel.

There were a lot of those lessons coming my way from my father, but our life was full of conflict and regret and ultimately split us apart after my parents divorced during my junior year of high school. He died from lung cancer when I was just twenty-three years old. I had for many years anger and some guilt for not repairing that relationship before his death. It didn't happen until I was in my thirties. Well, what the hell does this have to do with riding alone? It has everything to do with it, as I grew up with my parents' expectation that I would be the one to get things done and not rely on anyone else. My dad's lessons and my mom's moral support, simply put, made me an individual who knew that it would have to be me that got things done or obtained whatever I wanted. I learned through failure but also learned that self-reliance would produce the right actions that would impact the rest of my life.

So now we know how I got to this point in my life. My first touring bike was a scooter. What are you thinking? It's a scooter! At the time, when I told everybody that I was going cross country on a scooter, I got the usual comments about having to pedal with my feet, Fred Flintstone style, and was advised to get a real motorcycle. Bottom line, the BMW sport scooter is a 650-cc beast that could fly over a hundred miles an hour, get great gas mileage and compete with any other bike out there. I customized it with an eighteen-inch sissy bar with a four-inch round peace sign on the back to hold my gear. Two more bikes later and I have evolved to Yamaha's Super Tenere, one of the best dual sport adventure bikes on the road today. Its added weight, 570 dry, 1200 cc engine, comfortable seat and cruise control is all I need for my continuing journeys across our great, if politically divided nation. (I'm hating the word tribal.)

Being on a motorcycle is how I connect to being alone on the road and the earth I'm riding on. The Tenere's quiet, ruffled symphonic engine allows me to enjoy and HEAR what is going on around me. I find the noise of other bikes, and sometimes their riders, disruptive, and have always felt that it's how you get to your destination, not how you announce your arrival and what motorcycle you're arriving on. I don't begrudge anyone's choice of transportation but I get a little annoyed with the assumption that I own a Harley, an assumption that is usually made by people who have never ridden before but say that because of the great brand marketing brand Harley has done. Most commercials use Harleys in their production, but serious motorcyclists like myself may have had a Harley in the past and moved on to other makes because of their more reasonable upkeep costs, the exception being BMW and any Italian make such as Ducati, well-made bikes but with astronomical maintenance costs.

Gas Stations are Better than Technology

There are many great and sometimes puzzling results when gassing up your ride. There have been several occasions where I have found some incredible hidden treasures, which you have seen in my books. Usually the suggestion is "Oh, it's just down this frontage road" or "If you have some extra time." The latter happened in July of 2018 when I was on my way to Utah through Oregon via Portland on Highway 26 east.

I was gassing up around the half tank mark like I usually try to do. A fire service employee near his truck complimented my ride (which I bet he did quite often) and asked where I was going. I said Utah. He smiled and said, "It's a little out of your way just off the 7 north highway, but you need to see this huge gold and silver dredge in Sumpter; it's worth your time." He was right and a photo of it ended up in the book. The detour was about three hours but since I had no specific place where I was going to stay, it wasn't an issue.

Another example of a beneficial encounter at a gas station was trying to find the Cadillac Graveyard off Interstate 40 out of Amarillo, Texas. Again, the gas station network of information proved very helpful. I saw an out-of-state license plate close by and a family that looked like they would be stopping by all the possible tourist locations. I asked about the Graveyard and got a quick response. "Oh, it's just down this frontage road about a mile east of here." I was on my way west, frustrated because of massive road work in the area, but I wanted to see it so I headed east and there it was, spray cans and all. Those directions led to a shot and Haiku in book two.

A few times, though, my gas station ask for directions went south. While looking for a famous site, a well-hidden lawn tennis court in the middle of a corn field, outside of St. George City in Iowa, aka the tennis version of Field of Dreams, (only seen by one other person I've met), I got a local boy's "I have no idea" response. I asked this young motorcyclist, who was gassing up his dirt bike, if he knew where The All Iowa Lawn Tennis Club was. He laughed and said, "Dude, this is football country, people don't play tennis out this way, so why would I know about it?" I had a hunch that banks would know, though, and drove around until I saw a bank and pulled in. A few friendly tellers said "hello" and asked if they could help me. When I mentioned that I was looking for a grass tennis court, the two looked at each other, shook their heads and laughed, but a third teller heard and got the bank manager who went out of his way to help me out.

His response was somewhat typical of what you get when you're an out of towner from another state. "Just head out of town a bit, stay on the main rode which veers right at the gas station, continue on that road. When you see a car lot I think, or empty lot, take a right." Huh? I asked the name of the road and he said he didn't know. Despite having people from all over the world play tennis there, no signs gave you any idea that you were close or even on the way there. The bank manager failed to tell me it was down a graveled road "a bit." My standard tires on that bike, the Yamaha FJ-09, were not necessarily for gravel or off road travel. I shimmied down about a mile and a half, and there it was, with its three foot by four foot wooden sign just outside the court and your normal side vision view. A former feed lot, now a Wimbledon style tennis court.

The last treasure, my favorite, involved trying to locate a sixty-five foot original wagon wheel sculpture in yet another corn field, outside of Pella, Iowa. Pella, by the way, is the equivalent of California's Solvang, with its Danish bakeries, brew pubs and general stores that tourists flock to. In the center of the town square is Jaarsma Bakery. I just knew I had stopped by the right place for some calories and directions. It was packed. I asked one person in line for directions to the sculpture and four people replied. The only problem is that, at first, they thought I was talking about a bicycle tire sculpture where a major bike race was held a few years previously. But eventually the directions sounded solid, so I headed west of town and of course saw nothing on the road that resembled sixty-five feet. They said it would be on the right side of the road. I literally stopped and asked a jogger if he had ever seen my sixty-five foot wagon wheel sculpture. "No, but there's a sculpture just down the road. Yeah, it's a twenty-foot sculpture of bicycle tires." Gasp!!!!!

I headed north, disappointed and defeated. I saw a small highway on my Thomas map and headed east from there. Still reeling from the goose chase in Pella, I stopped for gas and reluctantly asked a person nearby about the wagon wheel sculpture. She responded no, but the other lady on my backside pump said it was just down that frontage road "over there" as she points north. My God, I'm a mile from it after spending two hours in Pella. I'm rolling my eyes and ask if it's the same sixty-five foot one I'm looking for. She responds "of course" but she had no idea how tall it is. I just needed to "head down the frontage road and turn right on the road with the T." Wow! I'm ecstatic. I finish my fill up and head down the sloping road only to notice that there seems to be about ten roads with Ts. You can't turn left because it's all corn. I think it was the fifth or six right turn down about a half mile and I finally see it. Another gem discovered either getting lost or getting gas station directions. Bravo.

I did have one unusual moment as I was leaving Wyoming in Lakota country where sometimes reservation territory paints a landscape of poverty and despair. An older man in a pickup came across the aisle to comment on all my gear. He asked me "Do you ever have any scary moments on the road?" My response was, of course, "Yes." The usual response from me referred to people changing lanes as they're texting, or just not even looking in their mirrors first to see my location, and also riding at night in the mountains because of deer and other animals. I've only had that happen a few times because I usually don't ride at night. He then asked, "What about those Injuns?" I paused before answering. I wasn't sure why he was referencing Native Americans as Injuns but by looking at his dilapidated truck and age, I decided not to comment. I assumed he'd driven through reservations many times during the day and at night a few times. His last comment was "At night, Injuns like to jump in front of your truck to end their misery, you know." He nodded his head a few times like a bobble head from a baseball stadium with a slight smile. He then added, "Be careful around here at night." He seemed sincere and I responded, "I'll do that."

I've ridden on a few stretches of reservation land myself and only felt uncomfortable once, when a poorly marked detour led me down a graveled road and after five miles I saw nothing but the sad and usual abandoned cars, empty buildings and wooden boarded-up windows on houses that I knew people lived in. Out of nowhere, a pack of big dogs from a property came right at me. Being in a graveled road with uneven foundation, without hesitating I hit the throttle, and kind spun out some, but was able to escape their pursuit. When I got to safety, I could only take a deep breath, feeling relieved that I didn't dump my bike and have to deal with that aggressive pack of canines.

One last note on that find in Sumpter, Oregon. I decided to gas up before I left town. Some small towns, of course, have one or maybe two gas stations. Some have just one pump, some just have unleaded gas for sale. It's Oregon, so they have gas station attendants to assist you. Most, if not all motorcyclists, like to pump their own gas for two reasons. 1. They don't want anyone banging on their gas tank or spilling gas on it and 2. In most states outside of California you can manipulate the nozzle, because they don't have preventative stoppers on them to keep you from doing just that, topping off your tank.

In Sumpter, the gas prices were, let's say, a tad high, like about five dollars a gallon. Getting between mid to high forties miles per gallon on my Tenere, I thought just one gallon would get me back to civilization. An older man came out saying I could pump my own gas. We were talking about the dredge and before you know it, the pump is at fifteen dollars. Wow. I had the five out when we started our talk. He just took the five and said to have a nice day. No way, that's ten dollars short. He gave me ten dollars of free gas. I will be making a full day's ride to hand him a signed copy of Haiku book number three, which will have the dredge in the book. That's the type of act of kindness that was the norm on this trip. Maybe I am just seen as an old man out on the road and appreciated for my enthusiasm and love of motorcycling. People are always willing to help if you ask and I also saw many people from tour buses and elsewhere posing by my bike when I came out from a store. Some even asked if their kids could sit on it for a picture. The hand-painted wolf on both sides of my gas tank started many a conversation and well wishes on my trip.

Special Thanks

To Linda Howey for the puzzle solving text I sent her to edit. I often type as a I am speaking to myself, as I am telling a story without worrying about sentence structure, punctuation and tense.

Canadian Big Apple Share

Play misty for me
Canada border neighbor
Tourists favorite

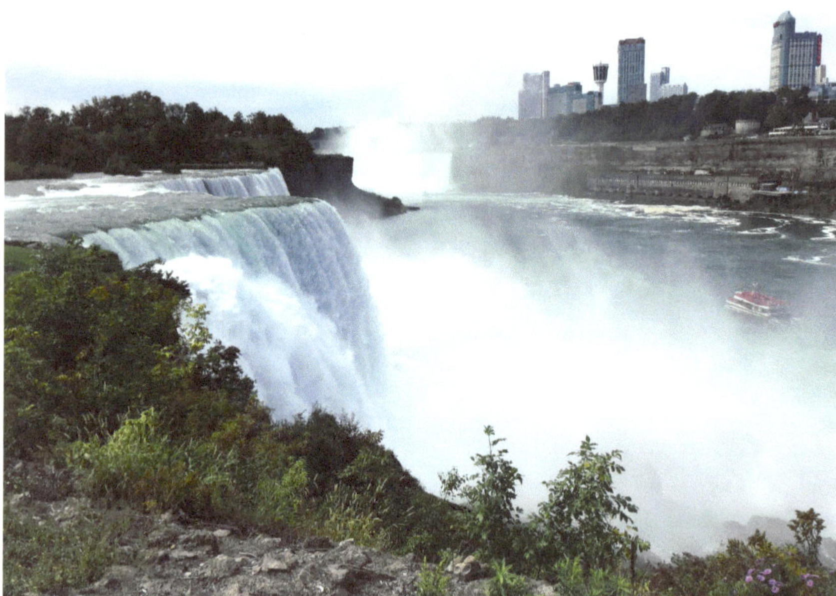

I'm not usually one to fight the crowds and photograph iconic landmarks but was glad I came to Niagara Falls which has a Canadian site as well.

Late Summer Rains

Calm after the storm
Trunks submerged sunset sunspot
Fall harvest waiting

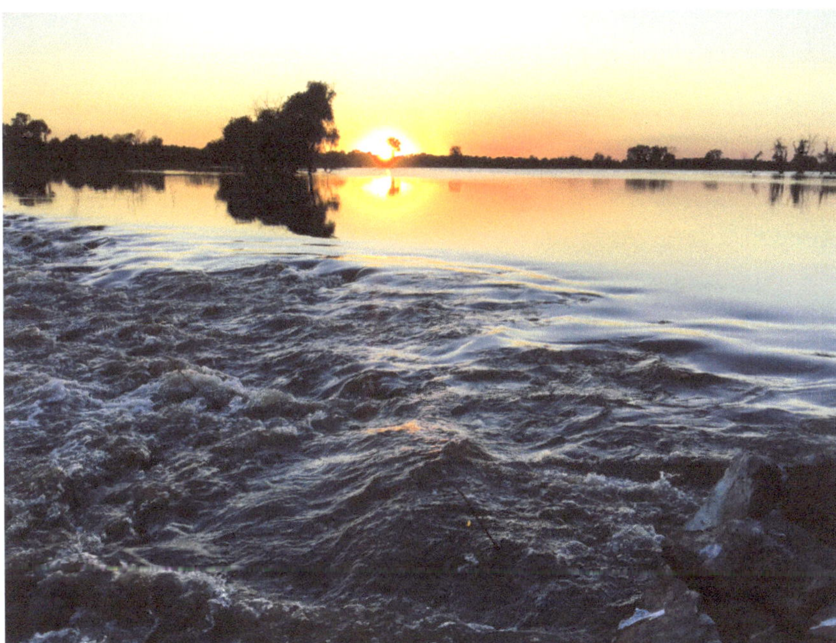

The weather is so unpredictable in the summer that fluke storms that can last for days, can cause delays for harvesting. Near Rummels, Iowa.

Bear Paw Surrender

Chief Joseph and tribe
Canada bound for freedom
Circled back but caught

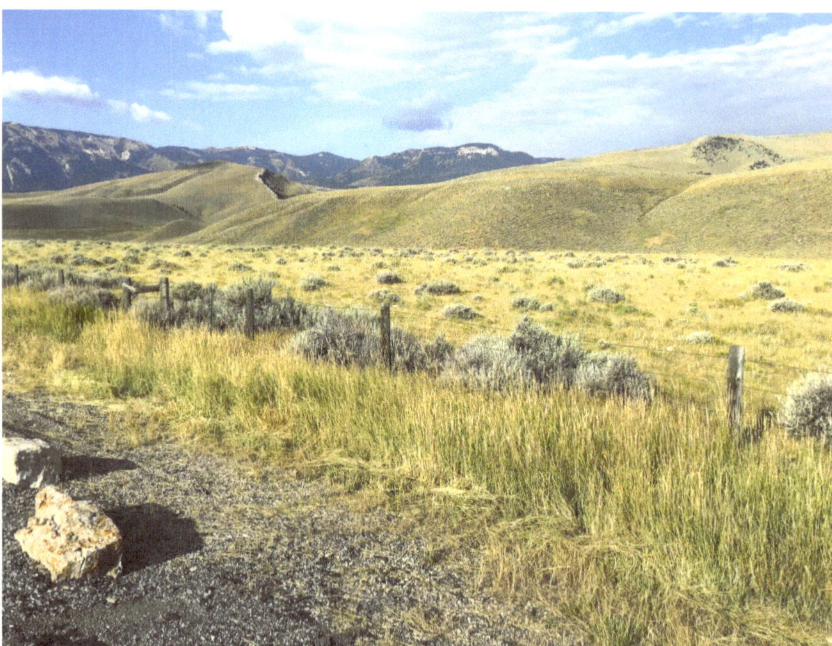

Chief Joseph and his Nez Perce Indians had temporarily fooled General Nelson Miles by circling behind them but got cornered and captured just forty miles short of the Canadian boarder.

Partners

Glacier perfection
Railroad bodyguard close
Traveling duo

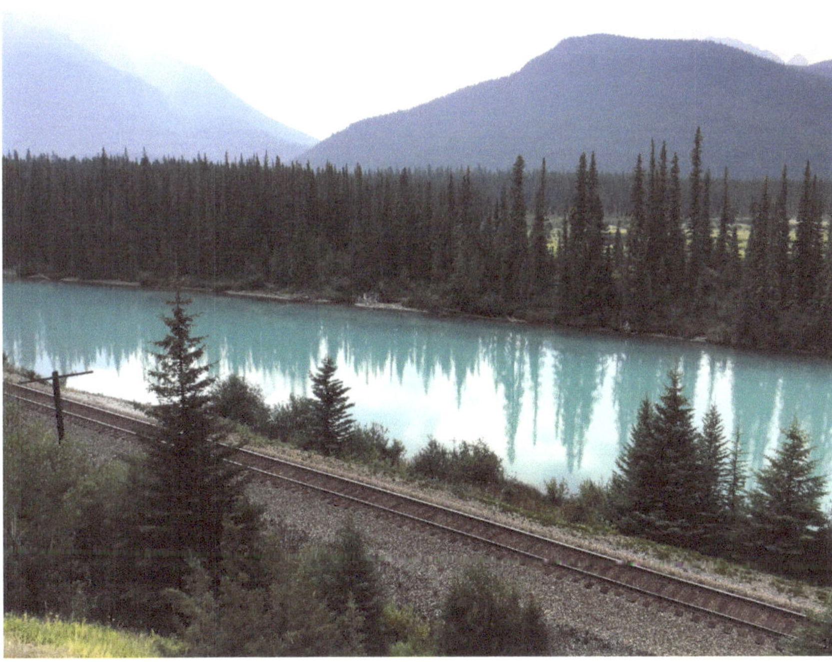

I often climb down from observation decks or hike off the beaten path as I am always looking for a different angle. This was no exception.

Neighbors

Walking bridge porthole
Reflections of autumn ponds
Black and white mirrors

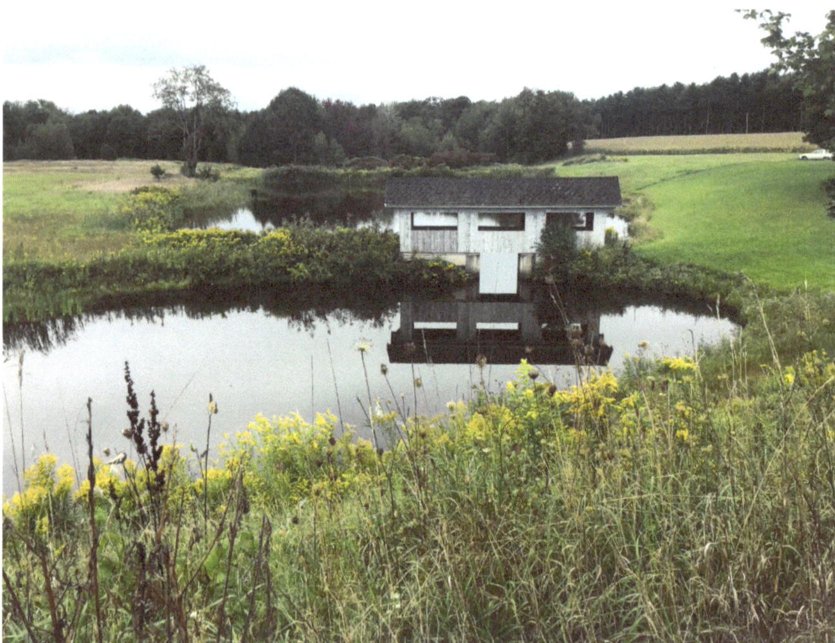

How fortunate I am to be able to travel America all times of the year and grateful for my partner Maggie who understands my incredible life on the road.

Dam it Up

Cascading rock flows
Lemoire River its power source
Boulders line its bed

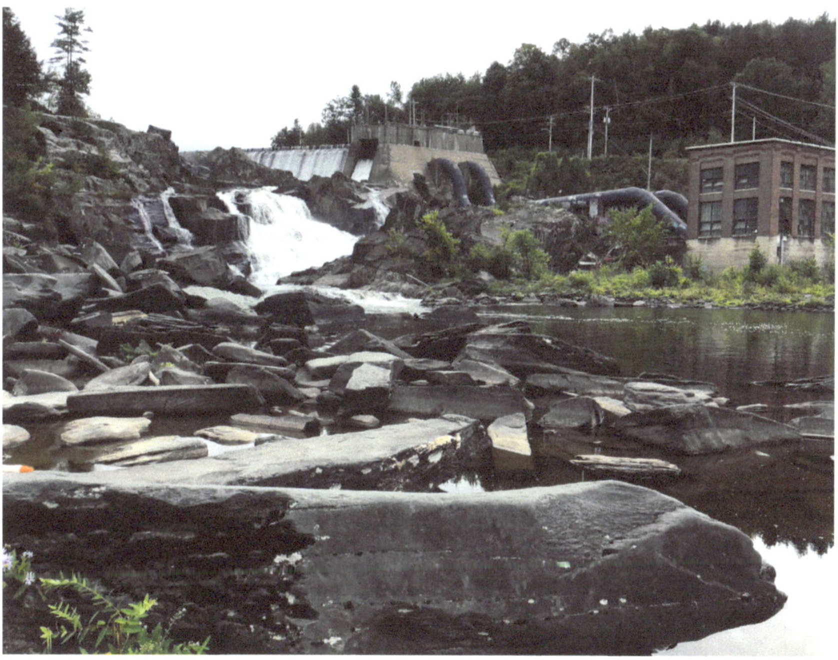

Another gem off Highway 104, Fairfax Falls is now a hundred years old and in the winter the vapors from the rocks above produce a mystic like mist.

Bear Tooth Bite

Sinuous journey
Forty degree icebox winds
Breath taking apex

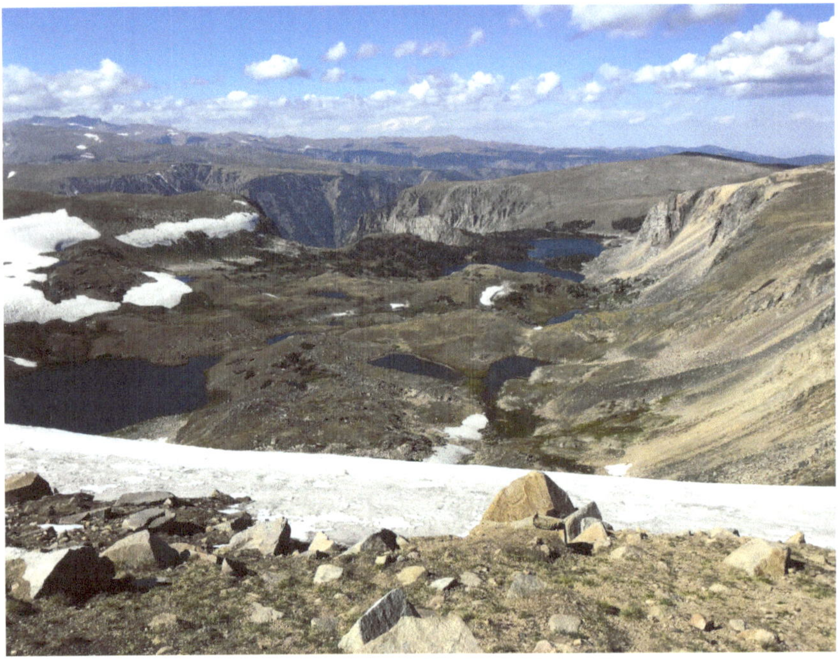

The Bear tooth pass was one of the most rewarding rides I have done. This is what I ride for. The results.

Broken Finger

Meandering path
Stream sizzlers through my valley
Gently lapping rocks

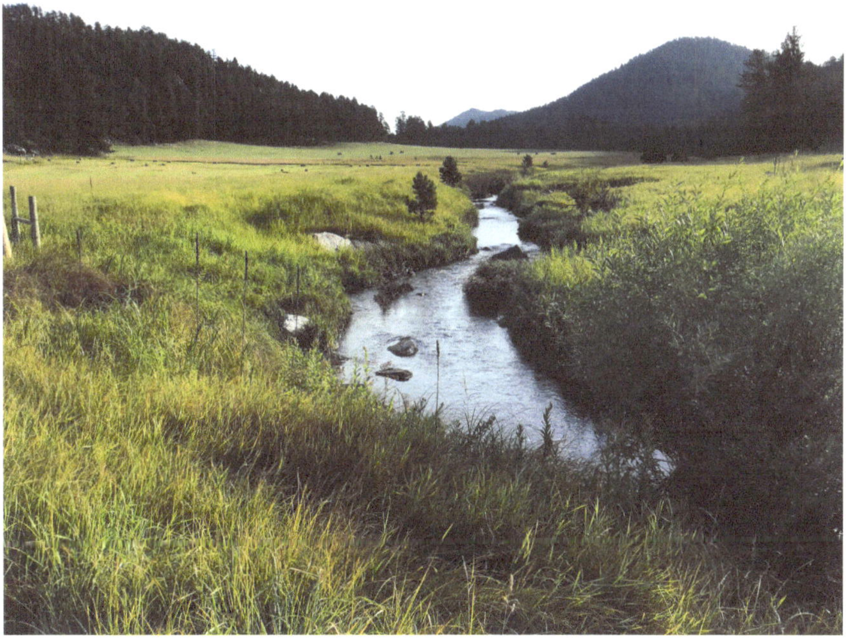

Custer State Park offers many opportunities for my lens and solitude time.

Mid Afternoon Canvas

Needled led pathway
Mount Olympus entry door
Pathway to heaven

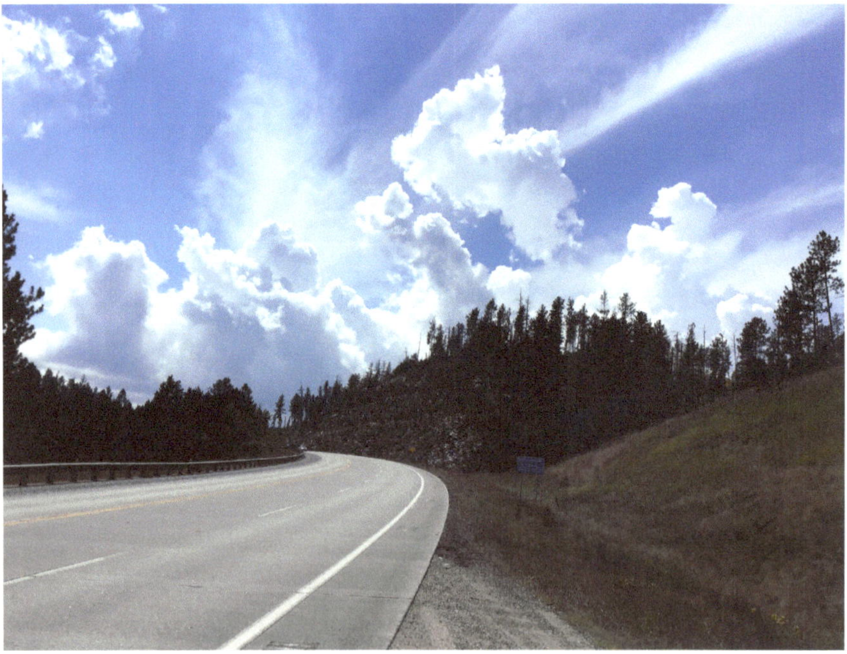

I seem to get a lot of road shots but you have to turn around to capture that exact moment that makes you brake. Ten minutes later, it might be gone.

Rest Stop

Open ranges for miles
Broken fences with barbed wire
Dreaming in the weeds

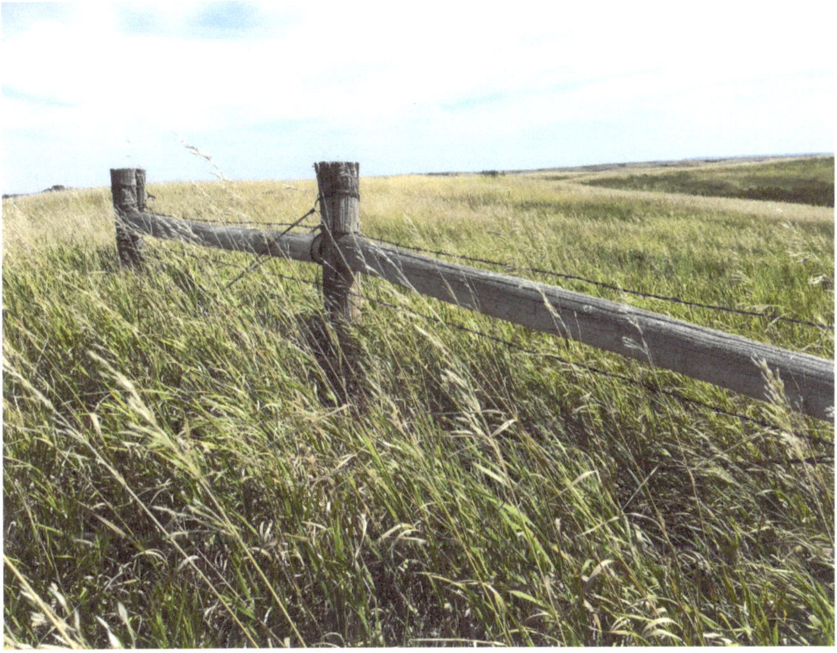

I've done this so many times on my journeys. My ride just off the road, my tank bag my pillow and my weary body snuggling the ground.

Dredging It

Scooping gold and silver
Bigger than a riverboat
Sumpter resting place

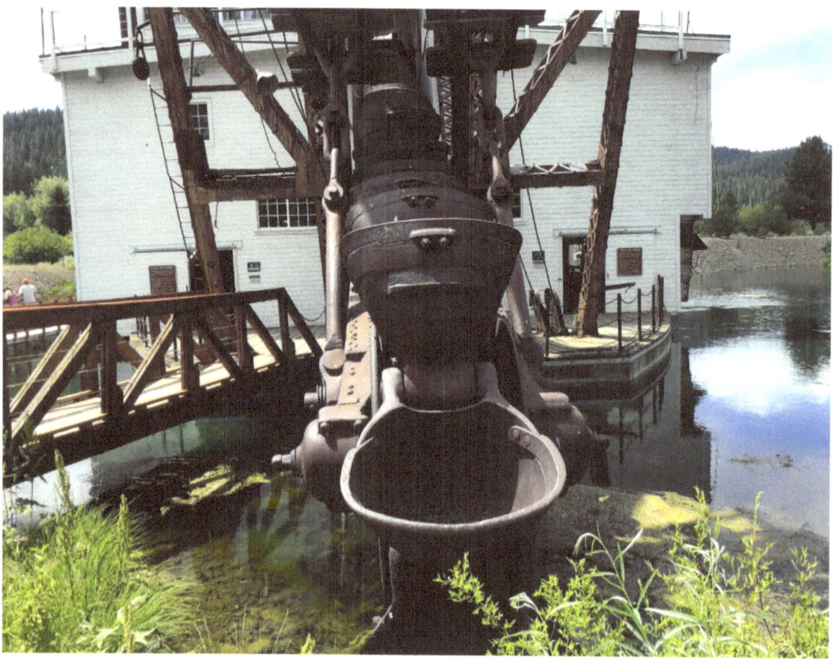

This massive complex engineering feat was able to dig its own way many miles to this final resting spot. Wish I could include all the shots from the inside. Well worth the effort off the beaten path on the 7 North in Central Oregon.

Receding Hairline

Glacier grinding rocks
Canadian Rocky home
Flowing mercy brown

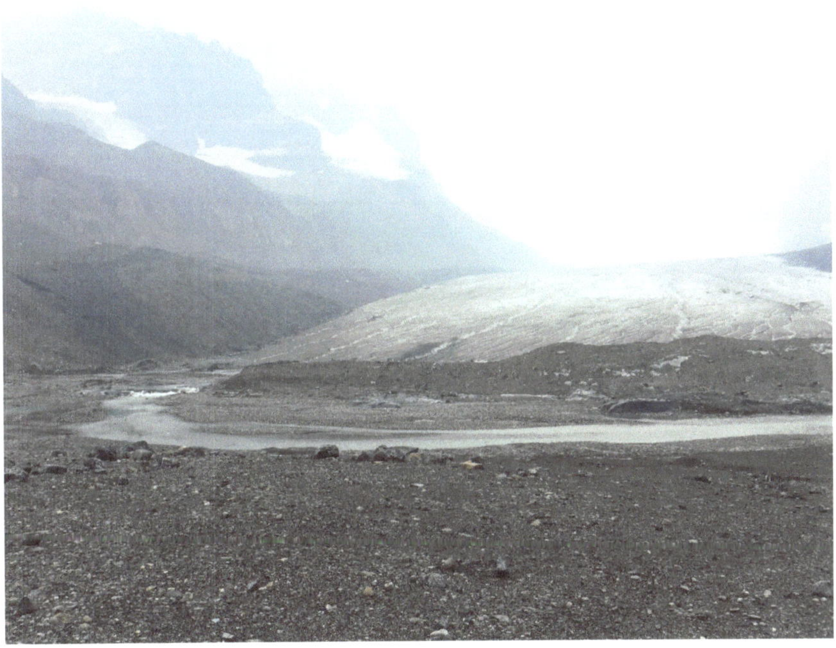

Glacier water can be dingy brownish or grey or brilliant green or blue turquoise in appearance depending upon the amount of grinding the rocks do when melting. Athabasca Glacier, just forty years ago, use to be at the bottom of the picture.

Steam it Up

Mountain climbing cog
Coal filled steam locomotives
Engineering feat

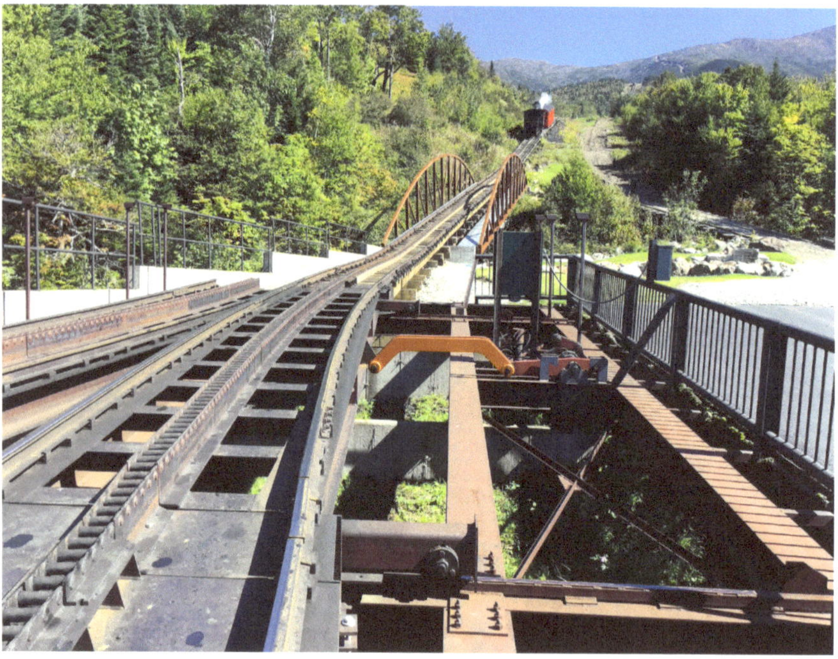

This mountain climbing cog locomotive is the first of its kind in the world and Mt. Washington, in the heart of its national forest, is its highest peak at 6,288 feet. Known as the worst weather in the North Eastern United States, its reputation for its notorious winds cannot be taken lightly, once recorded at 232 mph. Yikes!!

Run Cold Run Quick

Rambling into Park
Absoroka Range birth place
Yellowstone Lake home

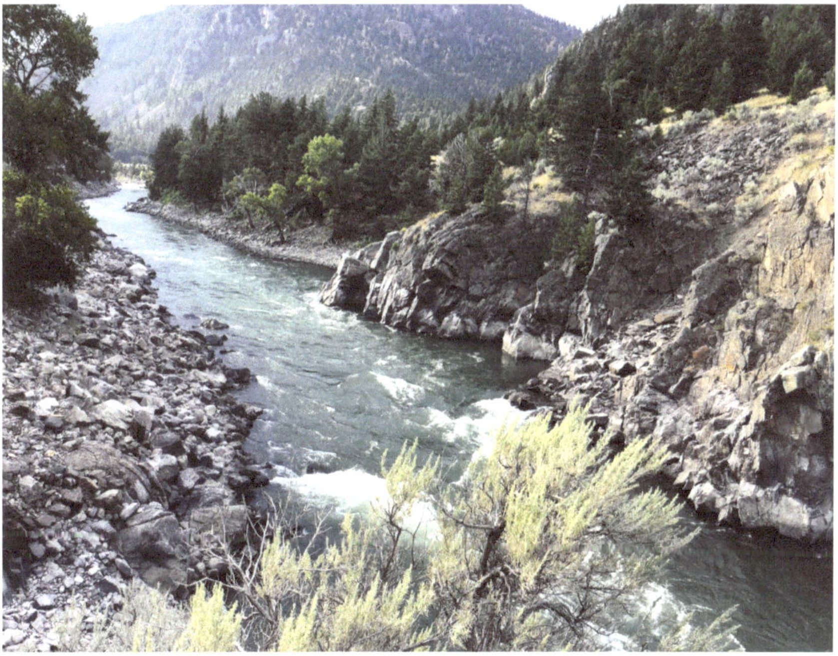

Even through twenty miles from the park, this river is very impressive.

Columbia River

Fourteen east first day
West coast burning up
Smoke not early morning fog

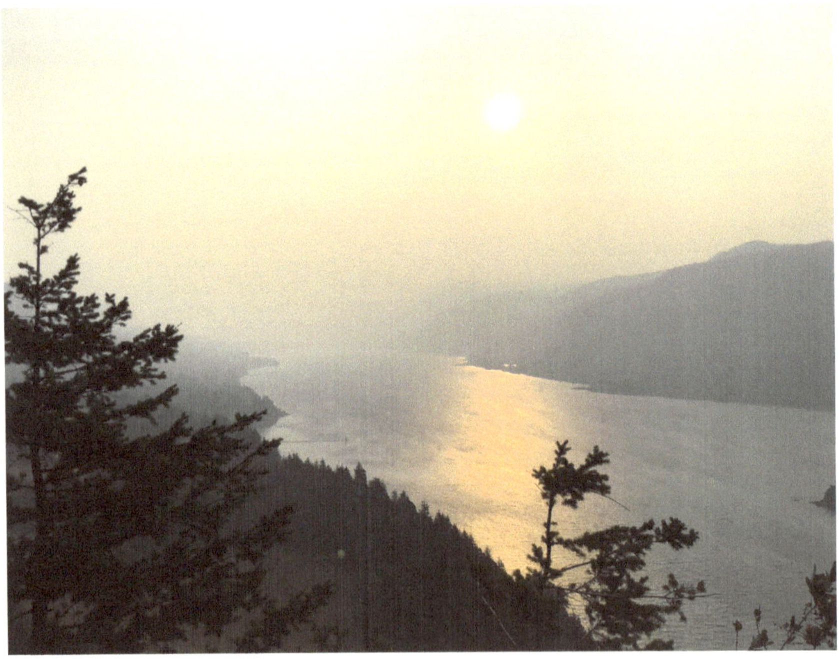

West coast fires pretty much followed me along with western Canada's fires the first week of this trip. I never saw the Canadian Mountains.

Old Vermont Mill

Stone lines entrance gate
Grinding grain in the old days
Wheel moved from river

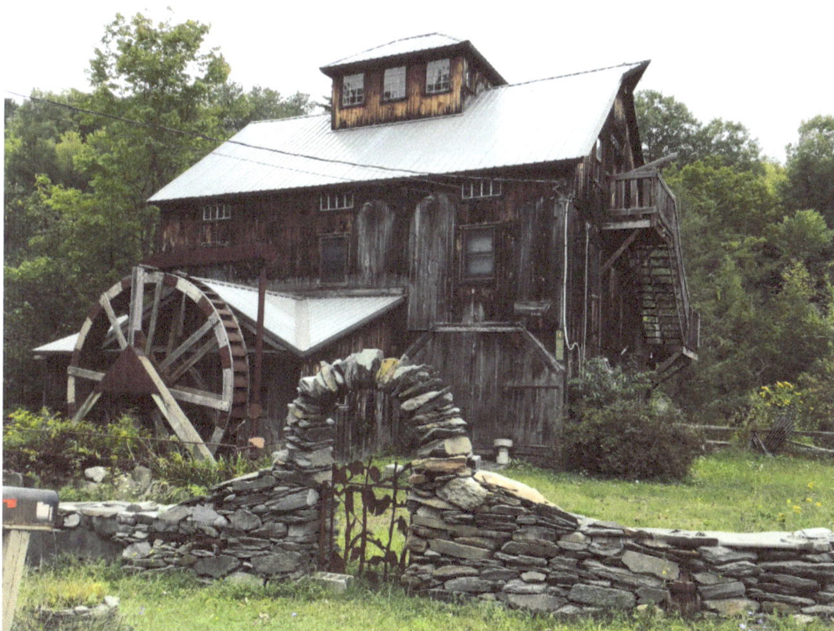

This structure looks older than it is. Built in the late 1970's it was a mill for a short time. Wheel moved up front when it became a restaurant but soon sold in 2003. Now locals say they only occasionally see a light on from its inhabitants.

Autumn on the Lake

Tree lined mirror pond
Golden bark reflects day
Setting afternoon

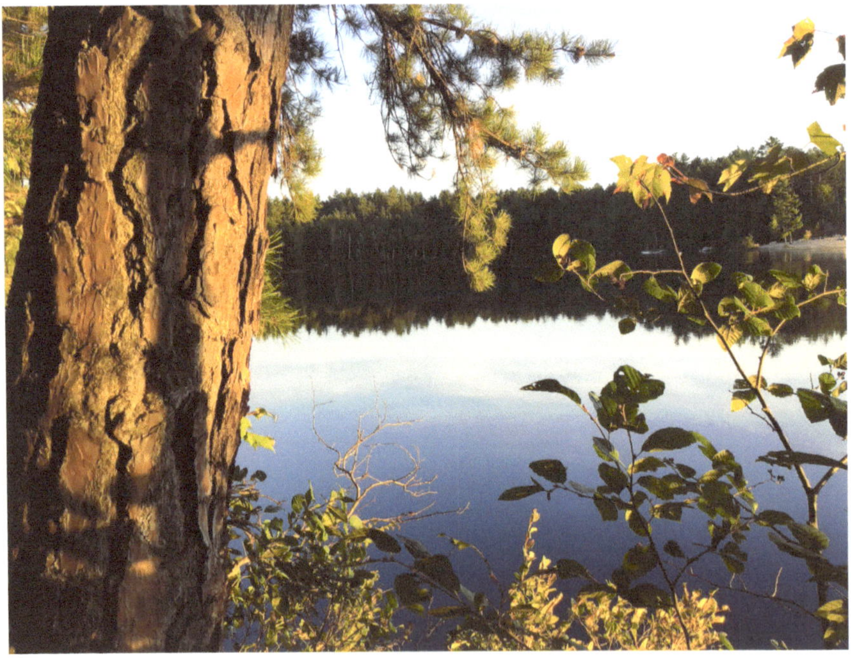

Hard to beat fall camping quiet after a busy fall weekend. Kids are back in school and you can go hours with your own thoughts.

John Day

Cloudless day alone
Late afternoon shadows cast
Silence in the hills

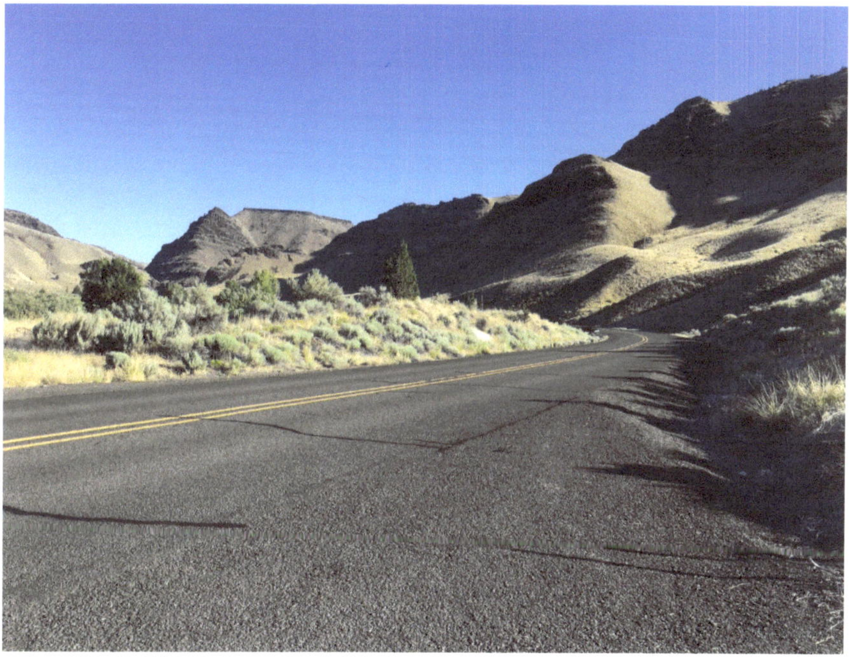

I love the late afternoon to shoot. This one from the John Day Fossil Monument Park in central Oregon. Literally by myself for an hour.

Mystic

Circles in the sand
Labyrinth paths of meaning
Chambers of balance

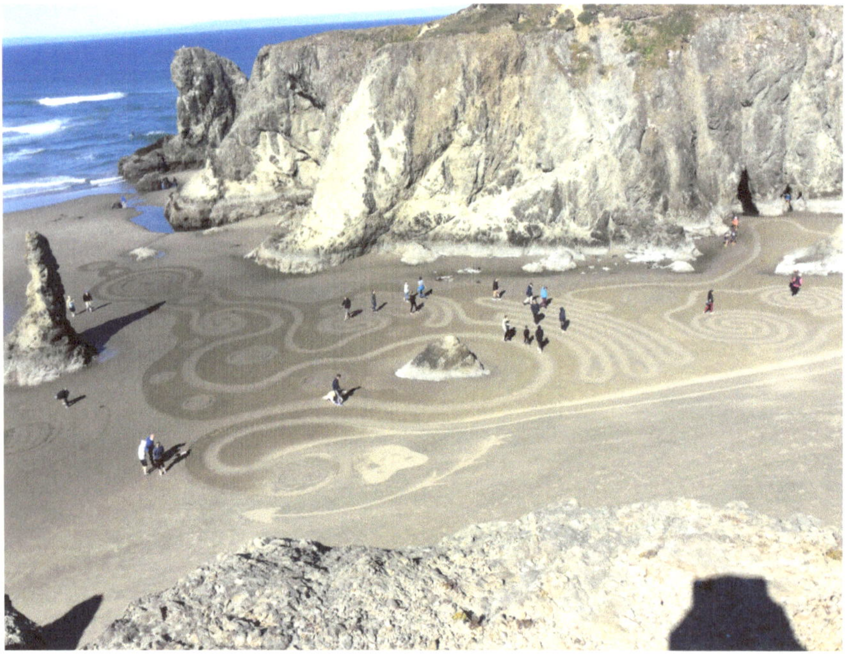

Off the southern Oregon coast, these drawings are subject to the tide schedule and only done at certain times of the month. Physically related to the inner ear of structure and balance.

Quiet Times

Miss you and the boys
Countless days away from home
Await your embrace

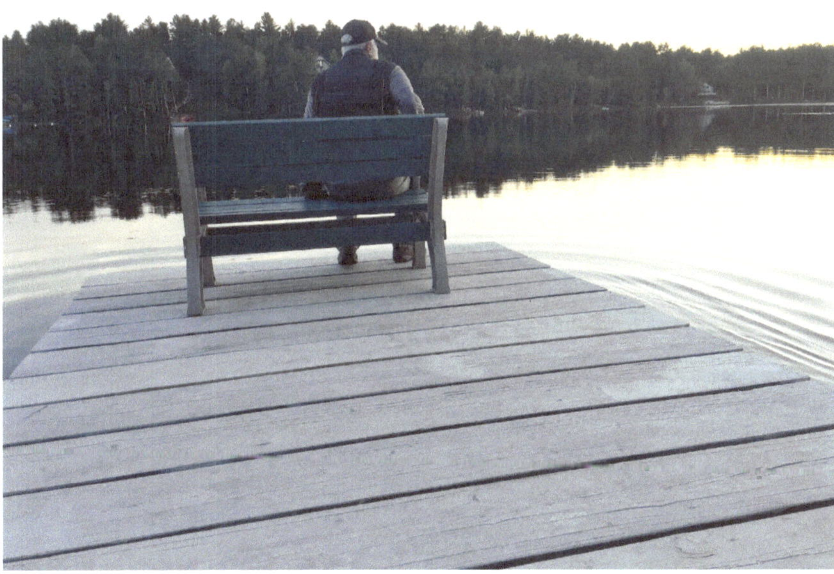

Motorcycling across the country is an incredible journey of surprises and rewards but can sometimes be arduous and exhausting. At times like this, it gives me pause to be thankful for what I'm coming home to.

Coconut Joe's

Working for the Man
Coconut shrimp ocean view
Isle of Palms our home

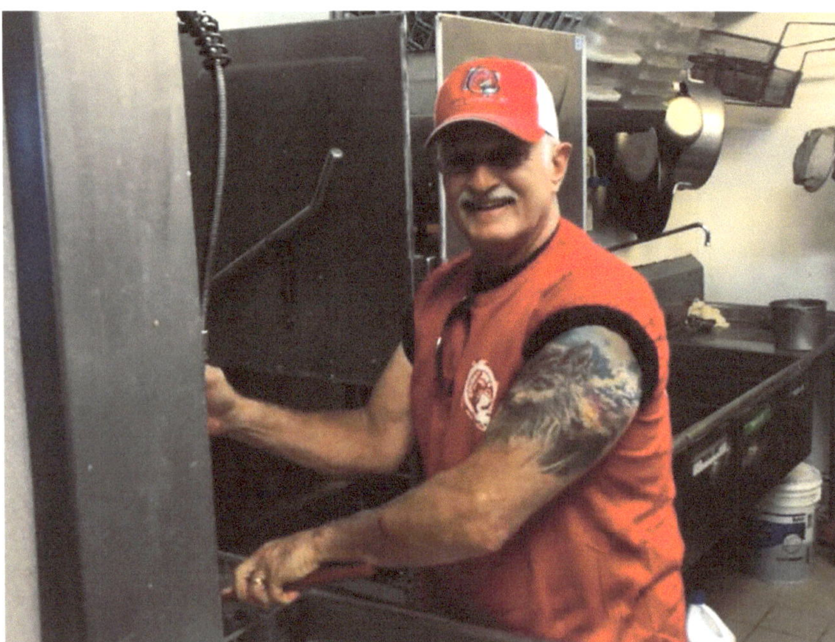

One of the most enjoyable elements of this trip was getting back in touch with old friends from Buena High School in Ventura, California. I've now washed dishes on both coasts. Ha!

Road Weary

In the weeds again
No emergency this time
Yet to be bitten

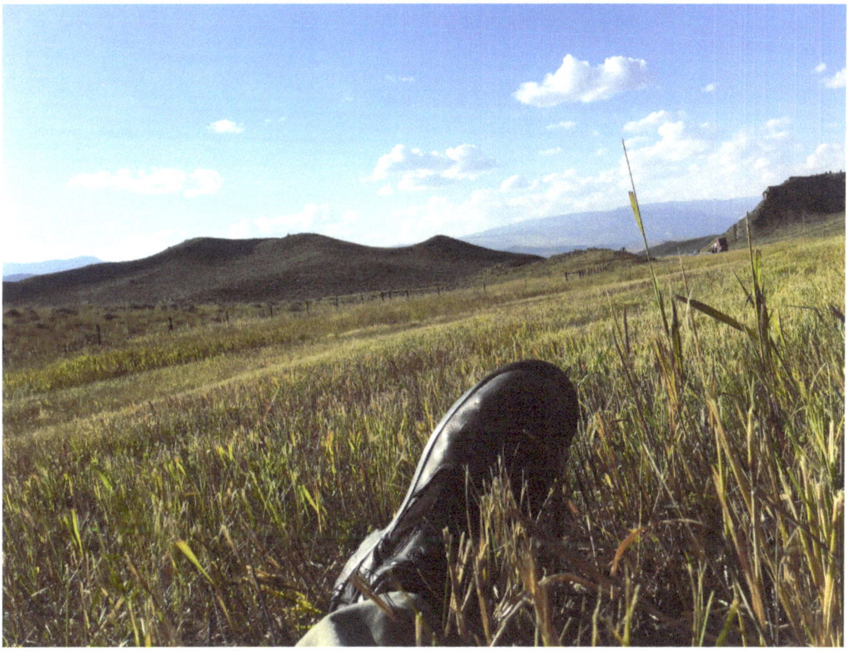

Instead of an EMT driver in a fire truck off Highway 101 checking on my status, this time it was a nice lady driver from UPS who wanted to make sure I was okay.

Whispering Cove

Carmel by the sea
Rugged coastline beauty stop
Year round treat to see

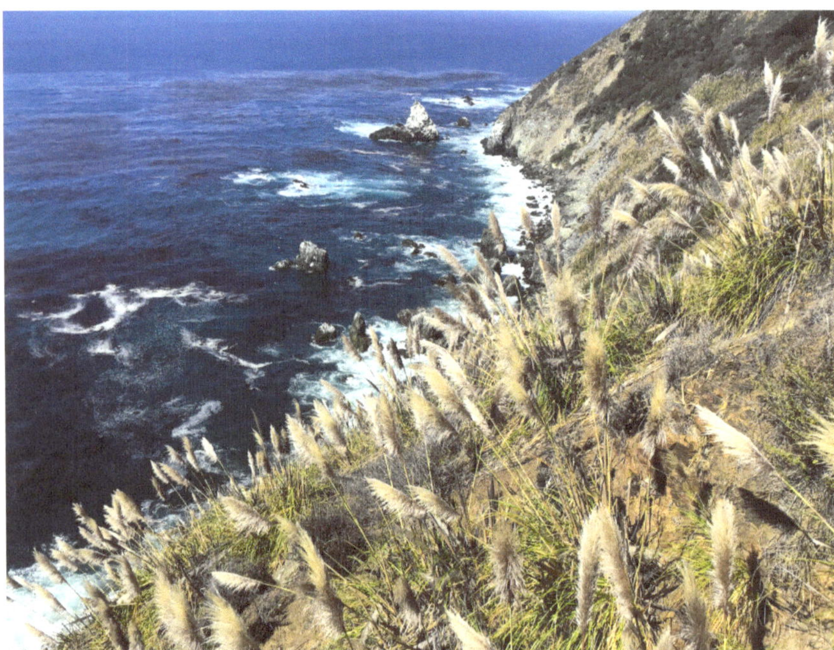

If possible traverse Highway 1 in the spring or fall where you'll not feel like your in traffic. The locals are more friendly and you see views like this.

Organ Tested

Endless washboard road
Stretches of navigation
Arduous entrance

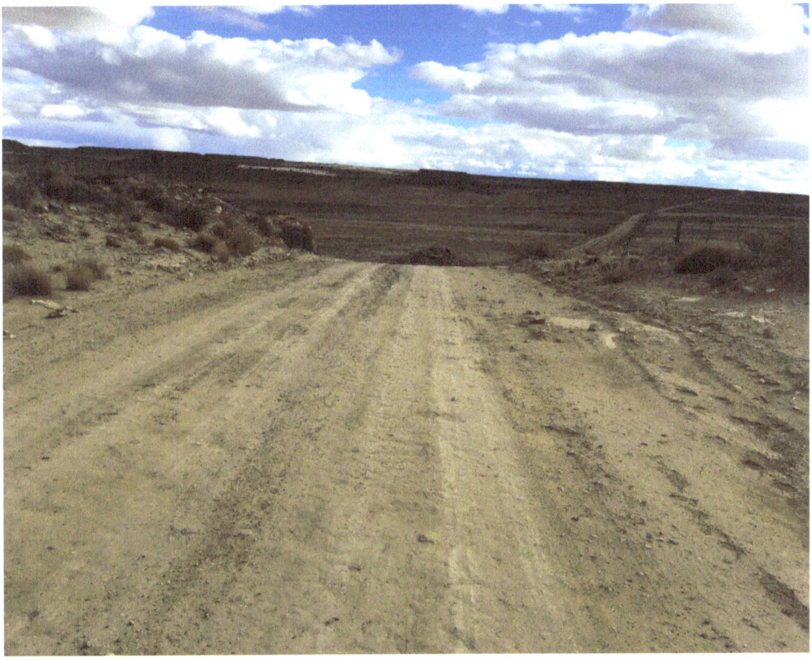

It may not look that challenging but the entrance and exit to Chaco Country is a theme park ride. After sixteen miles in and twenty miles out I felt like I was in a blender for margaritas. I almost dumped my ride after this spot dipped into a gully.

Highway 1

Jagged coastline view
waves slap rock community
mosses lichen thrive

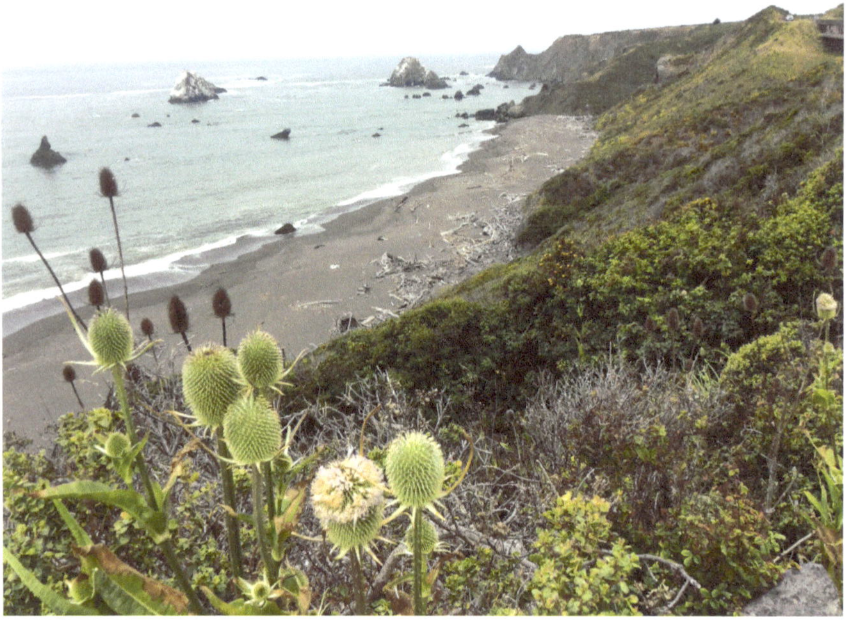

I love to hike and climb to get the desired shot. You literally have hours, miles, days and opportunities along the famed and much photographed Highway 1, California, USA.

Three Kings

Towering above all
Blooming in the springtime sky
Succulent giants

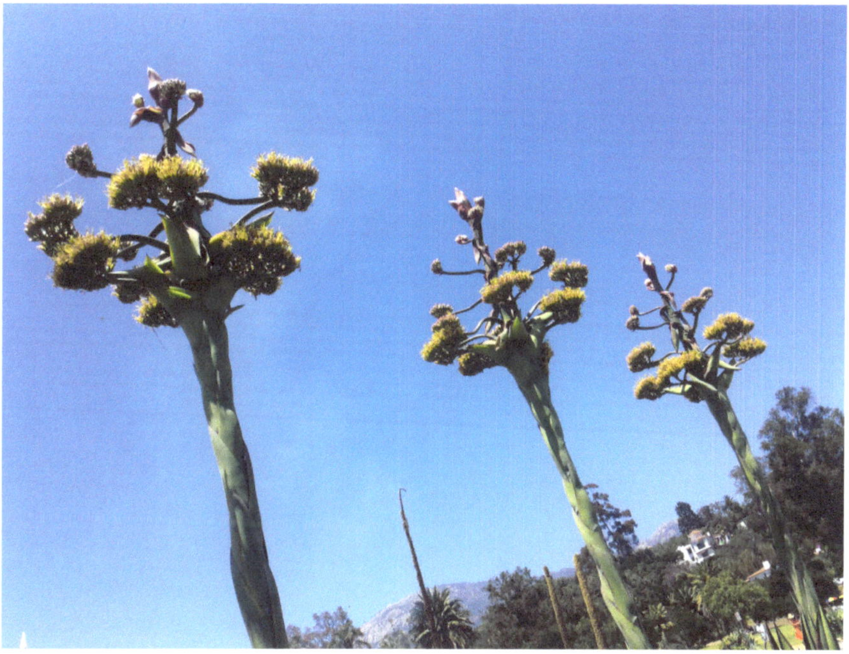

I've been to the Santa Barbara Mission quite a few times of the years but never one looked up before viewing the chalk drawings. These Arizona Agave were starting to bloom Memorial weekend.

Free Therapy

Carefree and happy
Saving thousands of dollars
Open road support

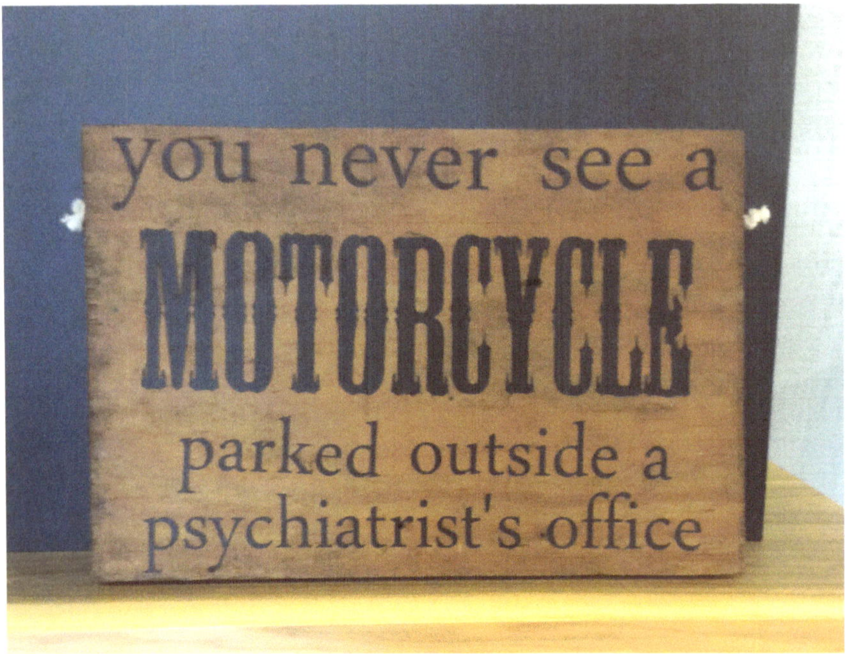

I've seen this sign in a few motorcycle shops on my travels. It always brings a smile to my face. No couch for me.

Hindu Temple

Peacock guardian
Elaborate furnishings
Urban Location

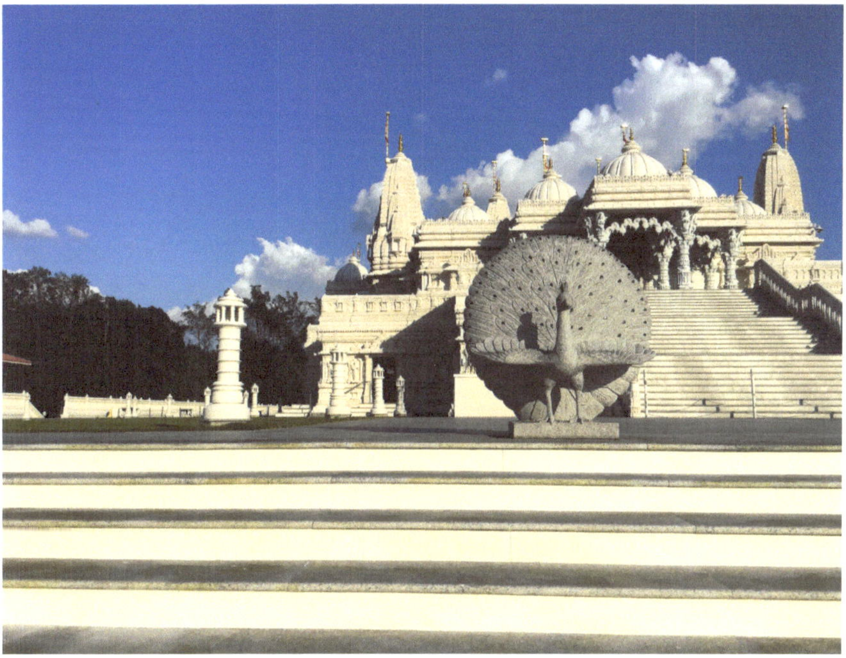

They place a awkward signs right in front of the temple so you can't really get a centered close up shot. When someone in South Carolina showed me the picture you would think you were in India. Not here, it's in Atlanta, Georgia.

Before the Battle

Early morning fog
Temporary sunrise cover
Field of battle soon

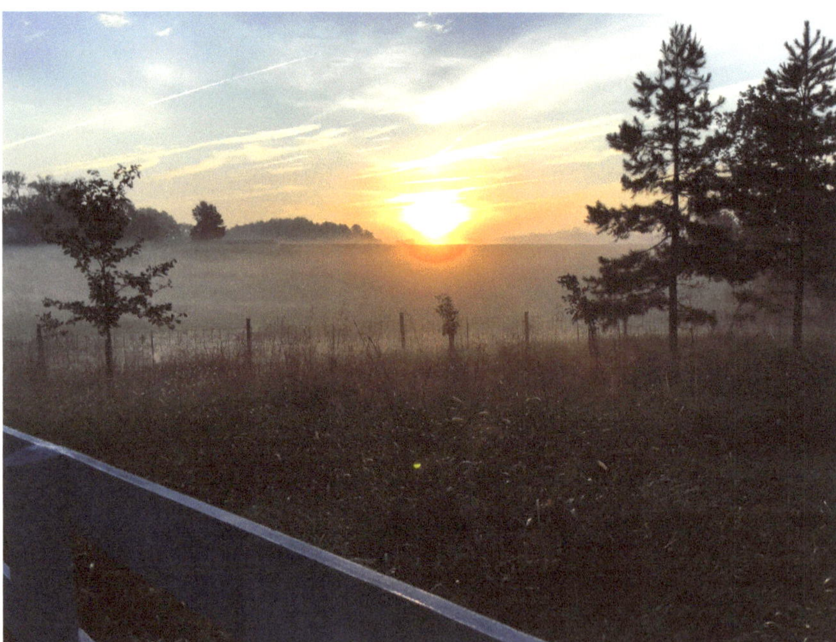

Virginia and other southern farmlands were the site of many bloody battles during the Civil War. As I departed outside of Charlottesville at daybreak this shot made me feel like I could have been there.

Better Times

Fifty years ago
Diners nostalgia hotels
Lost dreams Route 66

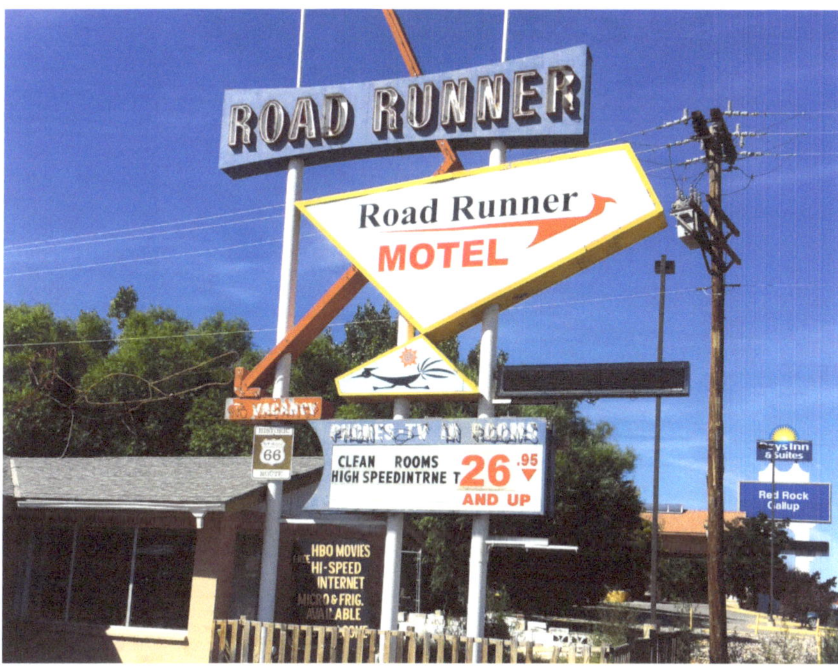

I've been on parts of Route 66 several times now and each trip I discover what progress and the Interstate program did to this gateway to California.

Chaco Culture

Astronomical
Solar and lunar cycles
Pueblo shale dwellings

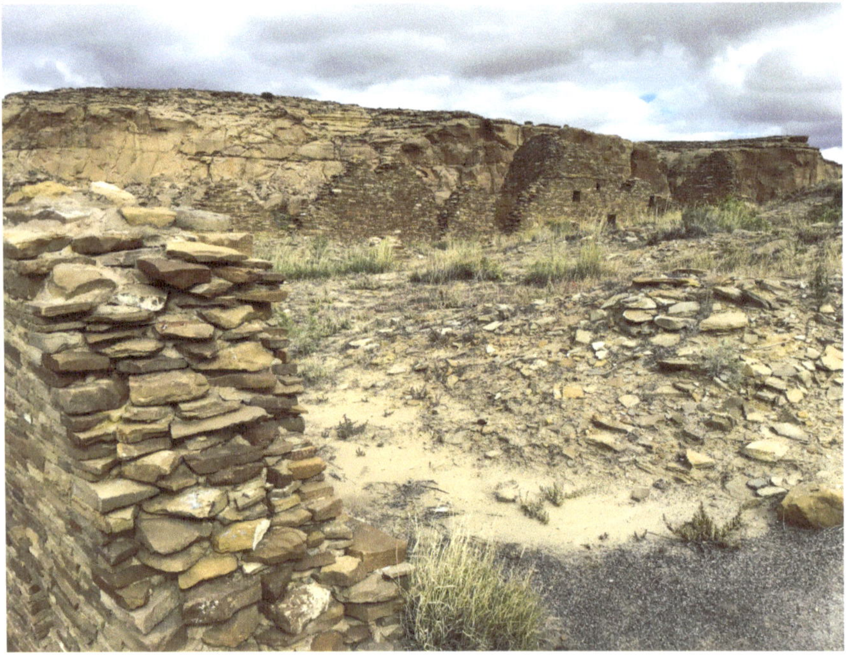

This Pre-Columbian culture has amazing mathematical designed structures that I hope next time I will get to explore more thoroughly. You need at least three days if you're a hiker.

The Audience

Black Hills gathering
Solo fans and families
Standing room only

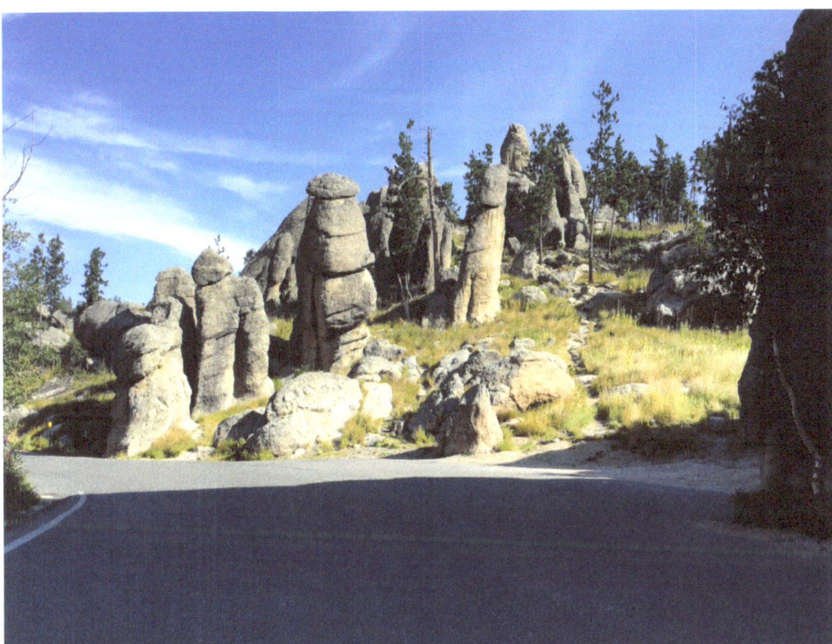

I wasn't expecting this crowd as I passed through The Needle in the Black Hills of South Dakota. They were waiting to hear stories of Lobo's travels.

Bad Gods Tower

White gypsum jacket
Laccolithic butte
Phonolite columns

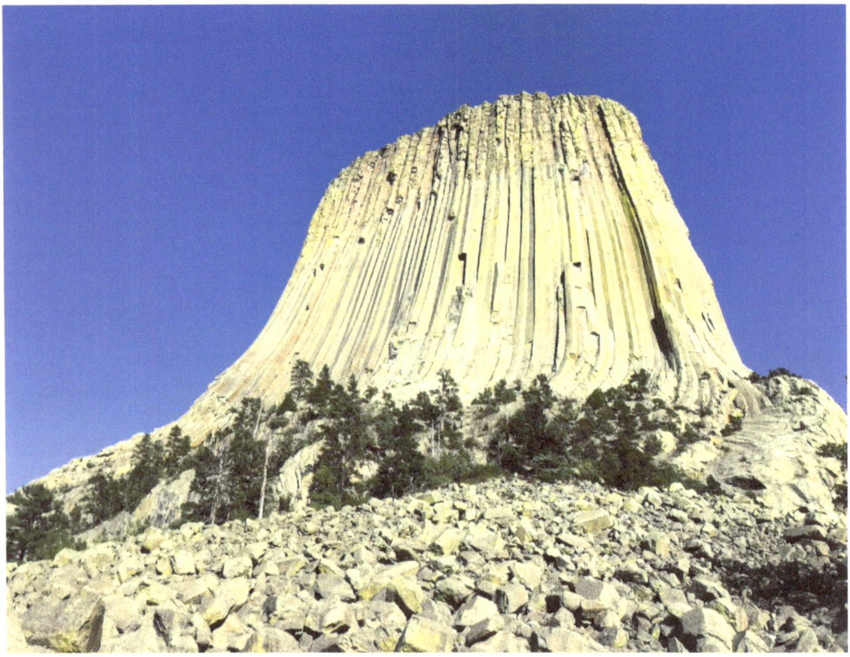

Lots of controversy trying to rename this site over the decades. I prefer to call it after what Native Americans would call it as opposed to The Devils Tower tag. I saw eagles flying above the rim. If I could, I would love to camp there one night.

Old Woodie

Grist Mill covered bridge
Small but intimate setting
Portal to get home

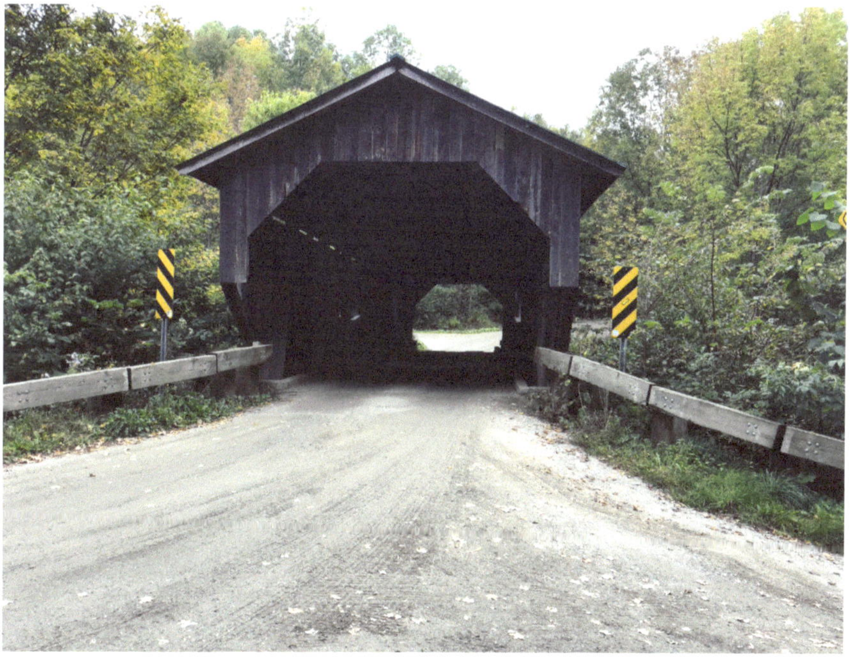

Built in 1884 in Jeffersonville Vermont, this bridge has no name posted on its forehead like most wooden bridges. Grist Mill is close by hence the name locals know it by.

Someday

Perhaps four or five
Anxious to get on my ride
Another Lobo?

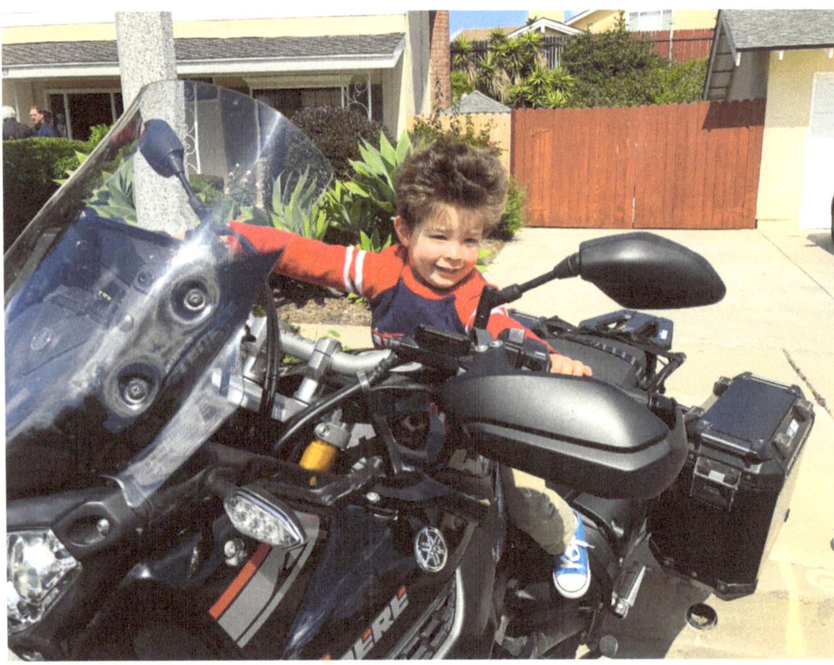

At a friends memorial last year, this kid reminds me of the circle of life. He has the same look on his face as I do everyday.

My Yamaha

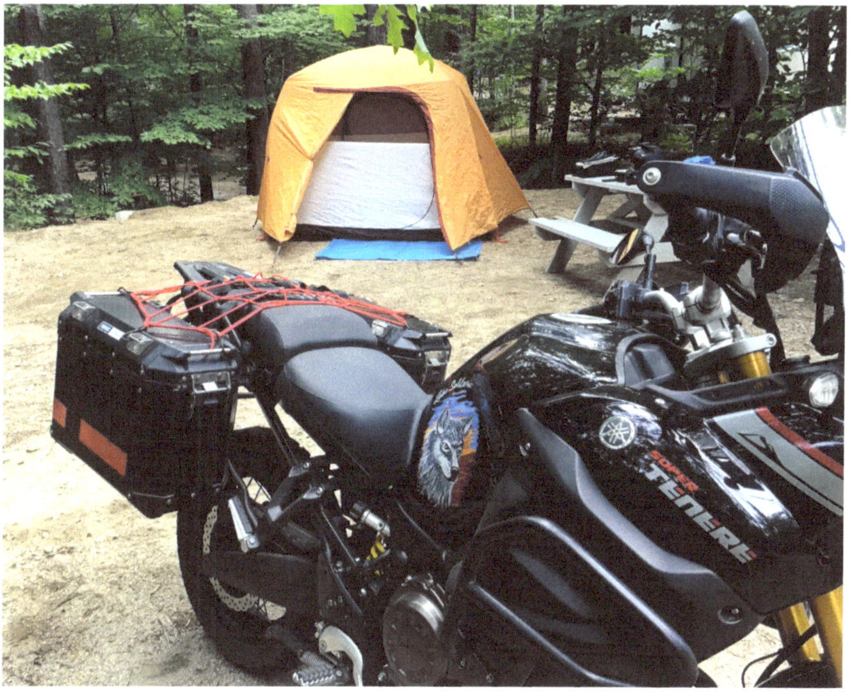

My Yamaha is an incredibly versatile motorcycle. Plenty of power, agility and is almost maintenance free. Whether I'm crushing the highways or being challenged off road, its dependability is expected. Definitely the best value for an adventure or as some call it, a dual sport ride. Thanks Wheels in Motion, and all their experienced staff in Chatsworth, CA for their knowledge and treating me like family.

Epilogue

There was a lot more preparation for this trip than I anticipated. I upgraded my camping equipment and rain gear and did a full service on my Yamaha Super Tenere, including new tires. With the ambitious goal of four months away from home, I knew there would be lots of adjustments to make along the way. One would expect this when traveling coast to coast, with a brief stop in smoky western Canada and its Glacier National Park, and regardless of the time of year, I'd be dealing with ever-changing weather conditions, poor driving habits of others and my biggest concern, animals.

You prepare for anything from freezing temperatures to triple digits. You expect road repair delays, waiting under bridges and at gas stations for severe and sudden storms to pass. I had about sixty pounds of camping gear and my morning serape for those camping days and famous napping in the weeds. If I just had a bulky mattress and a rocking chair on the top, I could appear to be granny from *The Beverly Hillbillies.*

In August, in western Canada, I was camping with temperatures in the low thirties and on Labor Day weekend I rode the Bear Tooth Pass outside of Yellowstone Park with temperatures in the low forties and forty mile an hour winds at 11,000 feet. On some of those sinuous turns I felt like a paper bag crossing the desert. That ride was one of the few times I bought a T-shirt commemorating my survival of a ride. Of course, at the apex of the mountain I saw a Canadian, according to the car license plate, wearing shorts, hat and a T-shirt. Dealing with that winding road in a car is a tad bit more doable than with a six-hundred pound motorcycle, sixty pounds of gear and a two-hundred pound fully geared up man. Geez.

Motorcycle Haiku is an incredible way for me to experience all the fantastic landscapes of America, especially those two-lane gems where I'm pumping my fist in the air when the conditions are perfect, and I'm on cruise control at seventy-one MPH in lane two and I'm basically the only one on the road regardless of the time of day. Many times, I saw no one in my side view mirrors for over an hour. My ideology for travel is simple. No itinerary, no reservations, no GPS and no "I have to photograph "a certain famous landmark and use an expensive camera to do so. *Motorcycle Haiku* is unique in that it has no plans or schedule, as every day brings new experiences that I can share with you through my lens. Keep it simple.

In conclusion, I would like to thank the ten couples along the way who were able to host me during this adventure. Their hospitality was embraced, as I never had to sit around a laundromat and I certainly enjoyed a few home cooked meals, which I savored. A few times I earned my keep, by washing dishes in South Carolina and mowing a massive lawn in Virginia. A few times I cooked for the family and there wasn't a day that I didn't think of my partner in life, Maggie Morrison, who during my absence had to endure our new puppy, Clemente, and do all the chores around the house I usually do, plus work full time. Maggie, you are wonderful and I'm lucky you support my passion for the road.

Fargosan

Just an old Beatnik
Many travels on two wheels
On two lane highways

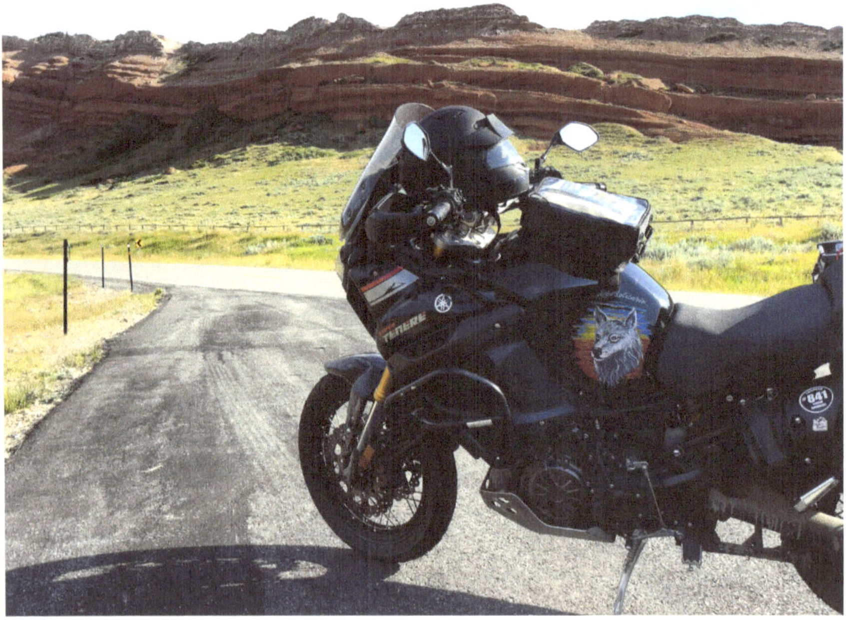

It just took a little nudging from two Japanese exchange students my last year in the classroom to motivate me into the Haiku world. Adding Haiku to my photographs, like motorcycling has changed my life.